Shelby County Iowa

Cemetery Records

FROM
CEMETERY READINGS OF
SHELBY COUNTY

COPIED BY
GRAVES REGISTRATION
W.P.A. PROJECT

Transcribed by

Diana Crisman Smith

HERITAGE BOOKS
2021

HERITAGE BOOKS

AN IMPRINT OF HERITAGE BOOKS, INC.

Books, CDs, and more—Worldwide

For our listing of thousands of titles see our website
at
www.HeritageBooks.com

Published 2021 by
HERITAGE BOOKS, INC.
Publishing Division
5810 Ruatan Street
Berwyn Heights, Md. 20740

International Standard Book Number
Paperbound: 978-0-7884-0954-7

Introduction

The Works Projects Administration contracted workers to complete a variety of tasks during the 1930s to help keep the economy moving albeit slowly.

In the State of Iowa, projects were undertaken in most counties to record the occupants of the cemeteries in the county. These projects were then prepared and provided to local repositories for reference.

These transcriptions were manually typed, with each county formatted as the project manager saw fit (except when the individual didn't follow those rules). The basic structure for this county (Shelby) was:
- Entries were alphabetical by surname, for the entire county.
- The surname was only listed once, with additional given names indented below the first of the surname.
- The name of the cemetery, and some indication of the location (usually township or town), were listed at the end of each entry.
- Some "comments" were included, often in parentheses, but sometimes just as an additional phrase within a given entry.
- Dates were listed inconsistently, probably in the style on the stone.

For ease of use and to deal with inconsistencies, the current editor has adopted the following standards:
- The entries are re-sorted alphabetically *by cemetery* to facilitate locating families of different surnames within a cemetery. The original gave no indication of location within a cemetery, so it is not possible to group adjacent burials. Some descriptive information has been added in the introduction to each cemetery, as well as notes on other names by which this cemetery is or has been known.
- The current editor has endeavored to locate burials for which the cemetery is missing in the WPA listing and assign to the proper cemetery. If not possible, they are included in an "other burials" section, which also includes some of the random entries for places other than cemeteries or cemeteries outside Shelby County.
- Some entries in the original WPA document included information other than name, dates, and cemetery location. Whether or not these notes actually appeared on the headstone is unknown. There is often an indication of "son of", "wife of," etc. For this volume, the following abbreviations have been used:

s/o = son of	d/o = daughter of
w/o = wife of	h/o = husband of

- Military service is also noted on some entries. The WPA copies were not consistent in recording this information, so the current editor has used the following:
  - A special symbol (ψ) has been inserted to highlight military service. Where the conflict was listed with or without the word "Vet" after, this work includes just the name of the conflict: i.e., Civil War, World War, Mexican War. [Note that this was created prior to the Second World War so any reference to World War is what is now considered World War I.] For some veterans (especially Civil War) the unit was sometimes also shown. These usually include the Unit (i.e., Co. E) and the branch (i.e., 32nd Ia. Inf.).
- Since the WPA document record dates are not recorded in a consistent format, the current editor has adopted the following convention. Dates are identified as Birth [B], Death [D], and/or Age at Death [Age]. Most are year only; if there is a full date, it is listed in the numeric format "mm-dd-yyyy";if it is a partial date missing the specific day, it is listed as "Mmm Yyyy", such as "Sep 1886." [No date] indicates that the WPA document was silent on the dates; (no date) was in the WPA document, implying no dates were found.
- Throughout the WPA transcription there were occasional handwritten notes, typewritten pages, or even document copies, inserted. These have been included with # before the surname.
- Comments by the current editor are included in square brackets [ ]. These usually indicate a guess at illegible, missing or contradictory text. Notes by the WPA project are in parentheses/round brackets ( ).
- Because there are so few cemeteries, most of which are VERY small, no additional index should be required. Simply scanning each alphabetical list of burials by cemetery is quick and easy to find a given surname. The majority of burials are in Harlan Cemetery.
- Not all cemeteries in the county were included in the WPA project. Some may no longer exist; some have changed names. Where available, this information has been included in the introduction to the section for that cemetery.
- These transcriptions were made in the 1930s (possibly into the early 1940s). The current editor assumes no responsibility for determining the accuracy or existence of the stones in the current cemetery.

INDEX OF CEMETERIES

Cemetery Name	Burials	Page
Astor Cemetery	51	8
Bowman's Grove Cemetery	0	6
Cass Township Cemetery	114	9
Clay Township Cemetery	0	6
Corley Cemetery	45	13
Cuppy's Grove Cemetery	4	14
Danish Cemetery	10	15
Danway Cemetery	36	15
Defiance Cemetery	3	16
Doyle Cemetery	11	17
Elk Horn Cemetery	3	17
Folck Cemetery	2	18
Galland's Grove Cemetery (RLDS)	-	60
Harlan Cemetery	1513	18
Jackson Township Cemetery	0	6
Jacobson Cemetery	0	6
Lapeer Farm	0	6
Latter-Day Saints Cemetery (LDS)	75	60
Lee Farm	4	63
Lincoln Township Cemetery	49	63
Merrills Grove Cemetery	25	65
Monroe Township Cemetery	2	66
Oak Hill Cemetery	3	66
Poplar Cemetery	10	66
Rabbit Hallow Cemetery	0	6
Red Line Cemetery	56	67
Rose Hill Cemetery	162	69
Shelby Cemetery	20	73
Slates Cemetery	1	75
St. Boniface Cemetery	2	75
St. Joseph Cemetery	4	75
St. Mary's Cemetery (Panama)	117	76
St. Mary's Cemetery (Portsmouth)	160	79
St. Peter's Cemetery	49	84
Washington Township Cemetery	77	85
Will Johnson Farm	0	6
Other Burials (Unidentified or out of county)	20	88

No burials were transcribed in the WPA manuscript for the following cemeteries, although they were listed in the table of contents.

- **Bowmans Grove Cemetery**

Located in Jacksonville, Center Township, Section 12. The cemetery is north of Highway 44, on the east side of Sequoia Loop.

- **Clay Township Cemetery**

Located southwest of Elk Horn, in Clay Township, Section 10. Cemetery is south of IA-173South, west on 500th Street.

- **Jackson Township Cemetery**

AKA: Bethlehem Lutheran Cemetery.
Located northeast of Jacksonville in Jackson Township, Section 17. Cemetery is north of 1000th Street, on the west side of Umbrella Road.

- **Jacobson Cemetery**

AKA: Rold Cemetery.
Located south of Harlan in Fairview Township, Section 26. Cemetery is east of US-59, south of 450th Street off Mulberry Road.

- **Lapeer Farm**

AKA: Altamont Church Cemetery.
Located in Clay Township, Section 11.

- **Rabbit Hollow Cemetery**

AKA: Rabbit Hallow Cemetery.
Located northeast of Harlan in Center Township, Section 4. Cemetery is north of Cyclone Avenue, off Nishna Avenue at Orange Road.

- **Will Johnson Farm**

Located south of Harlan in Fairview Township, Section 26. Cemetery is east of US-59, south of 450th Street off Mulberry Road.

Astor Cemetery

Located in Greeley Township, NW corner of Section 4. Astor WAS a town, but no longer exists. The cemetery is 1 mile west of Road M36 along the south side of the county line road (F16).

- ATHEY, Inez; D: 4-13-1904; Age 33; w/o D.R.
- BARR, Ethel Carange; B: 1886; D: 1917.
- BARR, Effie; B: 1833; D: 1912.
- BARR, George S.; D: 1-3-1894; Age 64.
- BARR, Jennie; B: 1862; D: 1916.
- BARR, Wellington M.; B: 1854; D: 1912.
- CADWELL, Lottie V.E.; B: 1877; D: 10-6-1895.
- CHRISTENSEN, Elsie Marie; B: 1828; D: 8-9-1912.
- CHRISTENSEN, Lena J. Fredricksen; B: 5-8-1867; D: 11-27-1908; w/o Kjeld.
- CRAKES, Emma; B: 4-13-1886; D: 3-8-1906.
- CRAKES. Phebe M.; B: 1843; D: 6-23-1898.
- CRAKES. William; B: 1823; D: 9-29-1896.
- DETWILER, Jacob L.; B: 1844; D: 7-1-1913.
- FISH, Elizabeth; B: 1841; D: 1917; w/o Isaac.
- FISH, Isaac; B: 1827; D: 1908; Ψ Co.H Mich. Inf.
- GLEISER, Alice F.; B: 1858; D: 4-10-1887.
- GLEISER, Carrie F.; B: 1842; D: 1914.
- GLEISER, John; B: 1851; D: 7-9-1919.
- GLEISER, Mary M.; B: 1847; D: 11-17-1906.
- GRIMES, Billy; B: 1914; D: 1932.
- GRIMES, Carl Wm.; B: 1890; D: 1918.
- GRIMES, Mary; B: 1857; D: 1937.
- GRIMES, Wm. Russell; B: 1848; D: 1916.
- HANNON, Anna Belle; D: 9-8-1886; Age 28; w/o C.M.
- HENRY, Ocean May; D: 3-30-1896.
- HOLMES, Charley; B: 1865; D: 1936.
- HOLMES, Thomas; D: 1-23-1898; Age 72.
- IVEY, James R.; B: 1879; D: 1916.
- JAMES, Alice H.; B: 1862; D: 1938.
- JAMES, Robert A.; B: 1857; D: 1932.

- JAMES, Sarah; B: 1836; D: 8-10-1901.
- JAMES, William; B: 1867; D: 1931.
- JENSEN, Mary; B: 1866; D: 1925; w/o Wm.
- JENSEN, William; B: 1865; D: 1915.
- LONGNECKER, William; B: 1847; D: 1916.
- OLSON, O.A.; B: 1862; D: 1936.
- PENNISTON, Edmund; B: 1845; D: 1925.
- PENNISTON, Mary Jane; B: 1852; D: 1917; w/o Edmund.
- RASSMUSSEN, Jensine; B: 1868; D: 8-10-1930.
- SLAGG, Nancy J.; B: 1856; D: 2-25-1892; w/o H.
- STEFFEN, Carl; D: 1-20-1900.
- STORY, Harvey W.; D: 9-13-1893; Age 32.
- SWENDSEN, Carl Alfred; B: 1879; D: 1934.
- THEOBALD, Isabella; D: 9-21-1886; Age 55.
- THEOBALD, Robert; B: 1819; D: 8-21-1900.
- TOMKINS, Annie; B: 1858; D: 1914.
- TOMKINS, Deborah; B: 1882; D: 1936.
- TOMKINS, Leslie E.; B: 1895; D: 1936.
- TOMKINS, Samuel; B: 1845; D: 1922.
- WEAVER, Al S.; B: 1861; D: 1929.

Cass Township Cemetery

Located southeast of Portsmouth in Cass Township, Section 27. Cemetery is south of Highway 44, east of Dogwood Road.

- ALBERTUS, John A.; B: 1863; D: 1932.
- ALBERTUS, Louisa; B: 1864; D: [1929]; w/o John A.
- ARNOLD, Jennie; D: 6-26-1892; Age 26; w/o of F.P.
- BAKER, Emma J.; B: 1852; D: 4-11-1894; w/o Milton C.
- BEAN, Nathaniel; B: 1844; D: 10-26-1897; Ψ Co.I 185 N.Y.
- BATTEY, Elizabeth A.; D: 5-28-1889; Age 19; w/o F.S.
- BAUERLE, Fred; B: 1863; D: 11-25-1891.
- BELL, "Father"; B: 1825; D: 4-20-1920.
- BELL, Elizabeth; B: 1857; D: 11-15-1907.
- BELL, Eunice A.; D: 9-17-1871; Age 37; w/o Thos.

- BENNING, Martha; D: 11-1-1894; w/o G.H.
- BENNING, Rosa Howe; D: 9-25-1896; Age 37; w/o W.F.
- BENSON, Bert; B: 1844; D: 1926.
- BENSON, Malena; B: 1845; D: 1919.
- BLAKELY, Rhoda E.; B: 1863; D: 1918.
- BOWMAN, Mary E.; B: 1864; D: 1934; w/o Sam'l.
- BOWMAN, Samuel; B: 1845; D: 1924.
- BREWSTER, Geo. H.; B: 1861; D: 1-28-1908.
- BREWSTER, Margaret; D: 8-20-1893; Age 73.
- BREWSTER, S.R.; B: 1853; D: 11-16-1917.
- BULLARD, Anna M.; B: 1831; D: 1899; w/o Jonathan (1st wife).
- BULLARD, Elizabeth A.; B: 1833; D: 5-6-1908; w/o Jonathan.
- BULLARD, Jonathan; B: 1828; D: 1913.
- CLARK, Elizabeth; B: 1867; D: 1930.
- CLARK, John W.L. (Dr.); B: 1825; D: 6-11-1881.
- CLARK, Joseph J.; B: 1888; D: 1928.
- CLAUSEN, Christena; D: 4-3-1895; Age 29; w/o H.
- COLEMAN, Sarah Ellen; B: 1880; D: 7-31-1912.
- COLLINS, Frederick; D: 10-7-1904; Age 81.
- COLLINS, Sarah; D: 2-22-1905; w/o F. Collins.
- COPELAND, Marietta; D: 9-6-1876; Age 22; w/o I. J.
- DAHLHIMER, Ellen; B: 1869; D: 6-21-1927; w/o John W.
- DAHLHIMER, John W.; B: 1865; D: 6-10-1910.
- DEUPREE, Daisy; B: 1879; D: 12-31-1930.
- DEUPREE, Lucretia; B: 1844; D: 12-21-1900; w/o William A.
- DEUPREE, William A.; B: 1845; D: 9-3-1898.
- DOHRMANN, Carl F.; B: 1856; D: 6-15-1917.
- DREIER, Anna; B: 1849; D: 1923; w/o Chris.
- DREIER, Chris; B: 1846; D: 1928.
- EGGERSS, Wilhelmine; B: 1835; D: 8-30-1923; w/o Carl E.L.
- EGGERSS, Carl E.L.; B: 1833; D: 7-7-1889.
- GERRATT, Ann; D: 12-15-1900; Age 82.
- GERRATT, Thomas; B: 1860; D: 1924.
- GILLESPIE, Angeline; B: 1846; D: 1931.
- GILLESPIE, Edwin A.; B: 1841; D: 1917.
- GOTTBURG, Carsten; B: 1820; D: 3-24-1885.
- GREEN, David; D: 11-21-1894.

- GREEN, Nancy Doner; B: 1840; D: 4-7-1914; w/o Wm.
- GREEN, Rachel E.; D: 4-7-1902; Age 85; w/o David.
- GREEN, Wm. F.; D: 6-16-1902; h/o Nancy.
- HALL, "Mother"; D: 2-23-1887; Age 79.
- HALL, David; D: 11-29-1913; h/o Emmaline.
- HALL. Emmaline; D: 11-26-1915; Age 72; w/o David.
- HALL, Joel; B: 1799; New Castle Co., Del.; D: 9-1-1882.
- HALL, Lula A.; B: 1875; D: 1919; w/o Alva.
- HALL, William D.; B: 1852; D: 11-24-1928.
- HALLIDAY, Alice; D: 2-14-1908; Age 85; w/o Henry.
- HALLIDAY, Henry; D: 8-3-1883; Age 57.
- HALLIDAY, Henry S.; D: 11-21-1886; Age 24; s/o H. & A.
- HAMMERAND, Fredericka; B: 1854; D: 9-2-1914; w/o John.
- HAMMERAND, John; B: 1853; D: 5-12-1889.
- HANDY, Martha; B: 1843; D: 9-1-1926; w/o Wm.
- HANDY, William; B: 1816; D: 8-11-1902.
- HELLYER, Amos; D: 2-27-1887; Age 48.
- HELLYER, Anna; B: 1841; D: 10-31-1898.
- HELLYER, Izri; B: 1817; D: 5-5-1891.
- HUGHES, Estella; D: 1-30-1900; Age 29; w/o C.A.
- HUGHES, Mary Ann; B: 1852; D; 1932.
- HUGHES, William F.; B: 1846; D: 1937.
- JOHNSON, James; D: 5-8-1900; Age 31.
- LAWRENCE, J.M.; B: 1844; D: 3-1-1923.
- LAWRENCE, Mary; B: 1860; D: 6-27-1906.
- LAWRENCE, Sam'l M. [no dates]. s/o J.M & Annie
- LAWRENCE, Sam'l P.; B: 1857; D: 8-19-1922.
- LAWSON, Leonard L.; B: 1859; D: 6-19-1894.
- LEYTHAM, C.H.; (no dates).
- LEYTHAM, Elizabeth; D: 9-26-1909; Age 80; w/o Richard.
- LEYTHAM, Richard; D: 4-10-1911; Age 88.
- McLILIER [?], --; D: 3-14-1896; Age 26; w/o W.H.
- MARLOW, Viola E.; D: 5-5-1917; Age 56.
- MARTIN, S.W.; B: 1847; D: 1923.
- MATHER, Elizabeth A.; D: 5-3-1891; Age 34; w/o J.H.
- ORRIS, Ella R.; D: 12-1-1902; Age 19.
- ORRIS, Joseph; D: 6-18-1888; Age 28.

- PEEK, Lillie E. Ely; D: 2-14-1882; Age 22; w/o C.L.
- POE, Anna L.; B: 1866; D: 3-28-1897.
- PUCKETT, Daniel; B: 1831; D: 7-22-1907.
- QUICK, Henry; B: 1833; D: 9-2-1913; Ψ Co.E 48th Ia. Inf.
- QUICK, Louisa; B: 1839; D: 7-9-1916; w/o Henry.
- QUICK, Susan R.; D: 1-24-1885; Age 31; w/o J.W.
- RANKIN, Cynthia A.; B: 1851; D: 6-3-1907.
- ROLAND, Jonathan; B: 1837; D: 7-15-1928.
- ROLAND, Sarah C. Cross; B: 1840; D: 3-26-1902; w/o J.
- ROLAND, V.S.; D: 6-5-1890; Age 29; s/o J. & S.C.
- SCROGGIN, Chas. S.; B: 1856; D: 1-26-1909.
- SEDDON, Joseph; B: 1848; D: 8-8-1925.
- SEDDON, Nancy H.; B: 1838; D: 1-3-1915; w/o Joseph.
- SLAVEN, H.C.; B: 1842; D: 1921.
- SLAVEN, Margaret E.; B: 1842; D: 11-5-1893; w/o H.C.
- SUMMERS, Martha H.; B: 1855; D: 1928.
- SWANSON, S.O.; B: 1847; D: 1928.
- THOMSEN, Peter; B: 1877; D: 5-3-1883.
- TURNER, George A.; B: 1-2-1899; D: 10-25-1918.
- VOGE (VOGUE), Lottie L.; B: 1868; D: 5-11-1934.
- WALMER, Anna M.; B: 1849; D: 1918.
- WALMER, Geo. Woodbury; B: 1848; D: 1918.
- WALMER, Lyle B.; B: 1875; D: 1929.
- WALMER, Mary L.; B: 1873; D: 3-5-1894.
- WALMER, Myrtle V.; B: 1875; D: 1927.
- WHALEY, G.A.; B: 1864; D: 1923.
- WHALEY, Louisa; B: 1833; D: 1-5-1893; w/o Valentine.
- WILLIAMS, J. Mae (female); (no dates).
- WILLIAMS, Josiah; B: 1856; D: 12-16-1894.
- WILLIAMS, William; D: 1-4-1882; Age 68.

Corley Cemetery

AKA: Fairview Township Cemetery.
Located northeast of Corley in Fairview Township, Section 3. Cemetery is north of F58, on the west side of Maple Road.

- ANDERSON, Chris; B: 1866; D: 1937.
- BROWN, Charity; D: 12-25-1871; Age 84.
- BURROUGHS, John G.; B: 1836; D: 1-28-1872.
- CARTER, Alice May; B: 1876; D: 4-14-1915.
- CARTER, Elizabeth; B: 1845; D: 7-20-1915.
- CARTER, Maud M.; D: 4-27-1896; Age 16.
- CARTER, William A.; D: 2-28-1900; Age 63.
- CUSHING, C. H.; D: 7-11-1892.
- CUSTER, Elizabeth; B: 1808; D: 11-27-1888; w/o H.
- CUSTER, Henry B.; B: 1807; D: 8-28-1885.
- CUSTER, Jane; D: 9-16-1916; Age 75.
- CUSTER, Rudy; D: 11-28-1899; Age 68.
- DUFFEY, Geo. M.; B: 1859; D: 5-9-1878; s/o J. & Lydia.
- FENTON, Paulina E.; B: 1845; D: 10-9-1874; d/o G. & E. Brown.
- GEAR, Mary; B: 1807; D: 1865.
- HACK, Albert; B: 1828; D: 6-29-1859.
- #HAMMER, Anna; D: 10-1-1873; Age 66; w/o R.
- HANSEN, Asmus; B: 1845; D: 2-4-1917.
- HAYWARD, Anne; D: 11-16-1882; Age 39; w/o Geo.
- HAYWARD, George; D: 11-24-1910; Age 72; Ψ Co.E 2nd Ia. Cav.
- HAYWARD, John; D: 2-18-1891; Age 82.
- HAYWARD, Lucy Ann; B: 1844; D: 7-5-1922; w/o Geo.
- KULLMAN, Augusta; B: 1853; D: 4-5-1934.
- KULLMAN, Fred; B: 1843; D: 1927.
- KULLMAN, Herman; D: 12-14-1904; Age 59.
- McGINNIS, Mary; D: 4-22-1901; Age 82; w/o Wm.
- McGINNIS, William; B: 1815; D: 1-20-1894.
- McKEIG, Emily E.; D: 1868; d/o W. & S.
- McKEIG, John Wesley; D: 5-2-1871; Age 50.
- McKEIG, Selma; D: 4-26-1874; Age 43.
- MANLY, Oliver O.; D: 11-6-1871; s/o A.J. & C.A.

- MANUEL, Frank; B: 1830; D: 5-9-1905.
- MANUEL, Mary; B: 1841; D: 3-14-1918.
- PRESTON, Clarissa M.; B: 1818; D: 4-19-1881; w/o Edw. B.
- PRESTON, D.E.; D: 11-7-1900; Age 53.
- PRESTON, Edward B.; B: 1812, N.Y. state; D: 1-30-1903.
- PRESTON, Emma J.; D: 5-15-1900; Age 34; w/o C.W.
- PRESTON, Mary (Mrs.); D: 12-26-1898; Age 70.
- RHODES, Mary; D: 4-14-1874; Age 47; w/o James.
- SHAFFER, Caroline; D: 6-29-1936; Age 86.
- SHAFFER, John J.; B: 1870; D: 12-7-1888; s/o L.K. & C.
- SHAFFER, John [Sr.]; B: 1811; D: 10-7-1889.
- TAGUE, Alexander M.; D: 3-23-1868; Age 43.
- WATERBURY, Catherine; D: 9-13-1875; Age 28.
- WATERBURY, Rachel; D: 3-21-1862; Age 20. w/o Lewis.

Cuppy's Grove Cemetery

AKA: Altamont Church Cemetery.
Located southeast of Harlan in Monroe Township, Section 7. Cemetery is south of F58 via Quince Road, on the north side of 500th Street west of Quince Road.

- KLINDT, Peter B.; B: 1870, Davenport, Ia.; D: 3-29-1935, Avoca; h/o Anna B. Samuels; Avoca Journal Herald, 4-4-1935.
- LEE, John Amon; B: 1870, Shelby Co., Ia.; D: 9-15-1922; h/o Susan M. Howlett.; Avoca Journal Herald, 9-21-1922.
- PIEFFER, Benj.; B: 1823, Pa.; D: 1-31-1899.
- SAMUELS, Milton M.; B: 1867, Racine, Wis.; D: 8-9-1929; h/o Louisa C. Sorensen.

Danish Cemetery

AKA: Olson Cemetery.
Located east-northeast of Shelby in Clay Township, Section 30.
Cemetery is on the west side of F66 east from Shelby.

- FROST, Anna Rasmine; B: 1862; D: 8-21-1880.
- HANSEN, Ingeborg; D: 6-21-1895; Age 62; w/o M.
- JACOBSEN, A.; B: 1839; D: 3-2-1915.
- JACOBSEN, Dorthea B.M.; B: 1845; D: 3-25-1901.
- JOHNSON, Denis.; B: 1861; D: 3-31-1923.
- JOHNSON, Olivia C.; B: 1867; D: 4-8-1900.
- LARSEN, Ferdinand; D: 7-28-1897.
- OLSEN, Peter; D: 4-28-1904.
- ROCKHOLM, Loren A.; B: 1863; D: 6-10-1904.
- ROGERS, Anna; B: 1844; D: 1-7-1893; w/o Christian.

Danway Cemetery

Located east of Kirkman in Polk Township, Section 19. Cemetery is just south of F32 east of Kirkman south to Timber Road, on the west side.

- AXLAND, Marcus; B: 1868; D: 1926.
- ERRETT, Julia; B: 1868; D: 3-18-1895; w/o T.R.
- HANSON, "Grandpa"; B: 1818; D: 1889.
- HANSON, "Father"; B: 1853; D: 1923.
- HANSON, "Mother"; B: 1850; D: 1911.
- HANSON, "Brother"; B: 1886; D: 1908.
- HANSON, Inar Reinhart; B: 1886; D: 1-4-1908.
- #HANSON, Martha K. (Johnson); D: 11-30-1914; Age 80 [60?]; w/o Emanuel.
- HEGLIN, Malinda; B: 1852; D: 1916; w/o Geo. G.
- HODNE, Dorthe Serene; B: 1876; D: 10-15-1909; w/o Carl.
- HODNE, Ellen Bargete; B: 1845; D: 9-28-1911; w/o H.P.
- HODNE, G. Peter; B: 1876; D: 1930.

- HODNE, Hogan P.; B: 1844; D: 7-21-1921.
- HODNE, Peder H.; D: 8-10-1919; Age 45.
- HODNE, Severt; B: 1889; D: 8-29-1919.
- JOHNSON, Anna; B: 1810; D: 5-5-1901.
- JOHNSON, Martha K.; D: 11-30-1914; w/o Emanuel Hanson.
- KNUDSEN, Bartha M. Hodnefield; B: 1864; D: 1923; w/o Hans.
- KNUDSEN, Hans; B: 1845; D: 1924.
- HANSON, Andrew; B: 1843; D: 1908.
- HANSON, Hannah; B: 1843; D: 1927.
- HANSON, Marseliys; B: 1842; D: 1905.
- MONSON, Cyrus; B: 1888; D: 1937.
- MONSON, Kasper S.; D: 2-4-1885.
- MONSON, Pauline; B: 1850; D: 10-28-1930; w/o Sven.
- MONSON, Sven; B: 1844; D: 9-3-1897.
- NELSON, Inger C. Thompson; B: 1873; D: 1932; w/o Tom.
- OLSON, Anna S.; B: 1858; D: 5-22-1892; w/o T.B.
- OLSON, Julia; D: 2-10-1916; Age 68; w/o N.
- OLSON, Nellie; D: 2-12-1891; Age 18; w/o O.N.
- OLSON, Nels; D: 1-20-1895; Age 58.
- SWETT, Regena Belle; D: 4-11-1894; Age 24; w/o A.D.
- THOMPSON, Christie; D: 2-6-1915; w/o Mons.
- THOMPSON, Geo. O.; B: 1879; D: 2-11-1899; s/o E. & C.
- THOMPSON, Mons; D: 4-18-1891; Age 74.
- WIGNESS, John; B: 1848; D: 8-12-1908.

Defiance Cemetery

AKA: Union Township Cemetery
Located northwest of Defiance in Union Township, Section 14.
Cemetery is north of 3rd Avenue on the west side of 5th Street.

- EIGLER, Joe; D: 9-30-1938; Age 83.
- KNO[A]USS, Samuel; D: 12-2-1910; Age 40; Res Defiance, buried there.
- YATES, Chas. Emmett; D: 1-7-1937, Council Bluffs Hosp; Age 75; h/o Lillian.

16

Doyle Cemetery

Located northwest of Earling in Grove Township, Section 28. Cemetery is west of IA37 via Dogwood Road south to 2080th Street west; cemetery is to the north of 2080th Street.

- JACKSON, Lafayette; B: 1844; D: 3-2-1868; s/o Lewis & Margaret.
- JACKSON, Margaret; B: 1816; D: 1-27-1856; w/o Lewis.
- KELLEY, Adam; D: 5-17-1879; Age 48.
- McDONALD, Amand; D: 4-3-1883; Age 43.
- McDONALD, C.W.; D: 4-20-1893; Age 62.
- PALMER, Catherine C.; D: 3-24-1874; Age 56; w/o J.H.
- ROUNDY, Asahel; D: 6-6-1878; Age 49.
- ROUNDY, Rena; D: 11-2-1880; Age 70; w/o Vriah [Uriah].
- ROUNDY, Vriah [Uriah]; D: 10-2-1869; Age 72.
- ROUNDY, Zebedee; D: 2-29-1855; Age 21.
- STRONG, Hannah G.; D: 4-11-1864; Age 38; w/o R.W.

Elk Horn Cemetery

AKA: Elk Horn Lutheran Cemetery.
Located north of Elk Horn in Clay Township, Section 1. Cemetery is east of Main Street (Hwy 173) on Elm Street.

- HANSEN, Jens Christian; B: 1849, Denmark; D: 7-4-1925, Atlantic.
- MORTENSEN, Nels Christian; D: 6-5-1920; h/o Anna M. Jensen; Buried Elk Horn, Ia.; Gutherian [Guthrie Center, Ia.] 7-6-1922.
- OLSEN, Thomas; D: 2-25-1938; h/o Olga K.; s/o Nels & Anna,

Folck Cemetery

AKA: Windy Knoll Cemetery.
Located southeast of Harlan in Center Township, Section 26. Cemetery is south of IA-44 East, then south on Quince Road. Cemetery is northeast off 800th Street.

- DUNCAN, Hannah. D: 1-31-1875 Age 74. w/o M.
- FOLCK, John. D: 5-4-1871 Age 74

Harlan Cemetery

AKA: Altamont Church Cemetery.
Located north of Harlan in Lincoln Township, Section 13. Cemetery is west of 12th Street/Linden Road, on the south side of Cyclone Avenue

- ABLAS, C.; B: 1-16-1835; D: 2-12-1891.
- ABLAS, Cathrina M.; B: 1839; D: 7-8-1914.
- ADAMS, E.T.; B: 1829; D: 9-23-1893.
- ADAMS, Abraham; (no dates); Ψ Mexican War.
- #ADAMS, James Henry; B: 1830, Canada; D: 2-22-1912, Idaho Falls, Idaho; Avoca Journal-Herald, 3-7-1912.
- ALEXANDER, Mrs. --; (no dates).
- ALLEN, Daniel W.; B: 1841; D: 4-23-1901.
- ALLEN, Edward Gerard; B: 1854; D: 9-22-1891.
- ALWILL, Agnes; B: 1857; D: 1928; w/o James.
- ALWILL, James R.; B: 1865; D: 1938.
- ALWILL, Martha; B: 1884; D: 1938.
- #AMES; George; D: 4-19-1939; Age 72; Burial Record.
- ANDERSON, A.P.; B: 1865 D: 1919. Ψ Spanish-American War.
- ANDERSON, Agnes. B: 1881; D: 11-10-1937.
- ANDERSON, Carrie Marie; B: 1877; D: 1920.
- ANDERSON, Charles; D: 4-2-1940.
- ANDERSON, Christ; B: 1850; D: 1931.
- ANDERSON, Ernest A.; B: 1913; D: 1936.
- ANDERSON, Isabelle Ferrel; B: 1850; D: 1930; w/o Samuel.

- ANDERSON, J.C.; B: 1861; D: 1929.
- ANDERSON, Julia Elsun; B: 1853; D: 1934.
- ANDERSON, Lue; B: 1867; D: 1935.
- ANDERSON, Mary; B: 1858; D: 1928.
- ANDERSON, Minnie J.; B: 1880; D:1899.
- ANDERSON, N.J.; B: 1850; D: 1938.
- ANDERSON, Nona Jeanette; B: 1887; D: 1917; w/o Emil.
- ANDERSON, Samuel; B: 1841; D: 8-10-1899.
- ANDREWS, Anna; D: 8-3-1891.
- ANDREWS, James; B: 1905; D: 1924.
- ANTHONY, Leroy F.; B: 1912; D: 1936.
- ANTHONY, Martin; B: 1862; D: 3-19-1933.
- ANTHONY, Mary; B: 1831; D: 11-17- 1907; w/o James A.
- ARGOTSINGER, Ora F.; B: 1892; D: 1928; Ψ World War.
- ARGOTSINGER, W. J.; B: 1856; D: 1928.
- ASQUITH, Sarah C.; B: 1848; D: 1924; w/o Theo.
- ASQUITH, Theo G.; B: 1841; D: 1924; Ψ GAR marker.
- ATKINSON, Elizabeth; B: 1816; D: 8-9-1905; w/o Jacob.
- ATKINSON, Jacob; B: 1807; D: 1891.
- B[ER]TKE, Minnie L. (Escher); B: 1882; D: 7-8-1922; w/o Wilson A.
- [BERTKE?]BURDKE, W.A.; (no dates).
- BABCOCK, --; D: 11-26-1938; w/o Joe.
- BABCOCK, Lrah [Leah]; B: 1817; D: 2-28-1900.
- BABCOCK, Lydia Jane; B: 1839; D: 12-4-1912; w/o Dr. L.D.
- BABCOCK, N.W.; B: 1809; D: 9-15-1889.
- BACON, Emeline; B: 1856; D: 1916; w/o Thos.
- BACON, Max E.; B: 1896; D: 1920; Ψ World War.
- BACON, Thomas; B: 1836, Ill.; D: 5-9-1909; h/o Emeline Miller.
- BAILEY, Horace W.; B: 12-7-1885; D: 6-7-1916.
- BAILEY, Robert; B: 1887; D: Oct 1934; Ψ World War.
- BAKER, --; B: 1888; D: 12-1-1927; w/o John.
- BAKER, J.A.; B: 1802; D: 8-2-1883; h/o Mary.
- BAKER, James Knox; B: 1835; D: 9-23-1907.
- BAKER, Mary; B: 1812; D: 4-9-1887; w/o J.A.
- BAKER, Milton C.; B: 1846; D: 2-18-1922; h/o Emma J.
- BAMSEY, John M.; B: 1870; D: 1935.
- BAMSEY, William H.; B: 1867; D: 1923.

- BARE, John; B: 1830; D: 1922; Ψ Co.F 24th Ia. Inf.
- BARE, Rachel; B: 1837; D: 1930.
- BARKMAN, David; B: 1839; D: 1915.
- BARKMAN, Nancy J.; B: 1847; D: 1915.
- BARNETT, Isabelle; B: 1826; D: 2-5-1897.
- BARNETT, Jame[s] C.; B: 1829; D: 5-6-1908; Age 79.
- BARTLETT, Beatrice H.; B: 1905; D: 1934.
- BARTLETT, Clarence L.; B: 1871; D: 1939.
- BARTON, Angelund; B: 1829; D: 12-12-1878; w/o Asher.
- BARTON, Asher; B: 1821; D: 1-12-1880.
- BARTRUG, Ed; (no dates).
- BARTRUG, Hallie; B: 8-29-1896; D: 4-25-1932; Ψ World War.
- BAUGHN, --; (no dates); w/o Harmon.
- BAUGHN, Alpha.; B: 1870; D: 8-23-1909.
- BAUGHN, Charles B.; B: 1856; D: 4-19-1891.
- BAUGHN, Harmon; B: 1840; D: 8-15-1912.
- BAUGHN, Herb; (no dates).
- BAUGHN, Luella Barton; B: 1845; D: 3-28-1930.
- BAUGHN, Urbana Adams; B: 1855; D: 9-26-1930.
- BAUGHN, Wilmot L.; B: 1850; D: 1-25-1917.
- BEAN, Thomas Henry; (no dates).
- BEARD, Roh[d]a B. (Lewis); B: 1837; D: 9-24-1922; w/o Albert.
- BEATY, D.W.; B: 1853; D: 1919.
- BEATY, Grover C.; B: 1885; D: 4-11-1908; s/o D.W. & E.
- BEEBE, Harry A.; B: 1881; D: 1939.
- BEEBE, James Albert; B: 1879; D: 5-7-1934; Ψ Spanish-American.
- BEEBE, Jos. E.; B: 1855; D: 1927.
- BEEBE, June C.; B: 7-7-1911; D: 10-7-1932.
- BEEBE, Mary Jane; B: 1857; D: 1927.
- BEEKMAN, H.A.; B: 1862; D: 1900.
- BEEMS, Sarah E.; B: 1851; D: 6-9-1910.
- BENFER, James; D: 3-31-1935.
- BENTEL, Elizabeth Moffitt; B: 1859; D: 1934.
- BERG, Katherine; B: 1861; D: 11-8-1881.
- BERGSHESSER, Aaron; B: 1811; D: 9-11-1880.
- BERGSHESSER, Catherine; B: 1825; D: 11-22-1869; w/o Aaron.
- BERGSHESSER, Susan H.; B: 1865; D: 8-22-1892.

- BEST, Carl L.; D: 11-17-1929.
- BIELETZKI, --; B: 1844; D: 1914.
- BIELETZKI, Carl A.; B: 1855.
- BILLINGS, Samuel; B: 1860; D: 1915; h/o E.L.
- BISGAARD, Chris; B: 1839; D: 1914.
- BISGAARD, May J.; B: 1845; D: 1922.
- BISGAARD, Peter; B: 1887; D: 1936.
- BISHOP, Anna; B: 1869; D: 3-28-1907; w/o J.H.
- BISHOP, Bertha Garland; B: 1878; D: 4-10-1904.
- BITTLE, Stella R.; B: 2-20-1890; D: 2-10-1918.
- BITTLE, Stephen; B: 1857; D: 2-14-1932.
- BITTLE, Elizabeth; B: 1867; D: 1-7-1924.
- BLACK, Perry A.; B: 1880; D: 9-16-1898; Ψ Spanish-American.
- BLAINE, Amanda T. Buchman; B: 1858; D: 9-30-1902; w/o A.N.
- BLAIR, J.P.; B: 1849; D: 2-9-1898; Ψ Co.C 47th Ia. Inf.
- BLAIR, June V.; B: 1900; D: 1928; w/o Gordon Sorenson.
- BLAIR, Louis; (no dates).
- BLAIR, Mary E.; B: 1875; D: 1927.
- BLAIR, Milton E.; B: 1877; D: 1921.
- BLAKELY, Ann; B: 1824; D: 11-6-1899; w/o James K.
- BLAKELY, James K.; B: 1822; D: 3-6-1899.
- BLAKELY, Princetta; B: 1859; D: 1930; w/o Wm.
- BLAKELY, William M.; B: 1855; D: 1929.
- BLAKLY, Arthur; D: 1929.
- BLIZZARD, Myrtle; D: 1-20-1891; Age 19.
- BLOCK, Harold; D: 1935.
- BOCK, Anna; B: 1832; D: 9-8-1899.
- BOCK, Bertha Thresa; B: 1885; D: 11-26-1907.
- BOCK, Christ F.; B: 1859; D: 1939.
- BOCK, Mettie K., "Mother"; B: 1856; D: 1926.
- BOCKEN, Henry; B: 1862; D: 1936.
- BOCKEN, Herman; B: 1887; D: 1934.
- BOCKEN, Josephine; B: 1859; D: 1928.
- BOHAM, Peter; B: 1853; D: 1927.
- BOIESEN, Christina; B: 1840; D: 2-7-1896.
- BOLLERMAN, Anna; B: 1836; D: 1909.
- BOLLERMAN, C.H.; B: 1834; D: 1912.

- BOLLERMAN, Frank N.; B: 1876; D: 1899.
- BOMBERGER, William Moore; B: 1856; D: 1923.
- BONE, Gertrude Sybil Hunt; B: 7-23-1886; D: 9-11-1917.
- BOOK, Christ; (no dates).
- BOOK, Emma, "Mother"; B: 1857; D: 1932.
- BOOK, Frank, "Father"; B: 1840; D: 1915.
- BOOK, Harry; B: 1877; D: 1926.
- BOOK, Ruth V.I.; B: 1892; D: 1936.
- BOOTH, Mary A. Phillips; B: 1850; D: 1936; w/o Nathaniel.
- BOOTH, Mary Prudentia; B: 1858; D: 2-6-1903.
- BOOTH, Nathaniel; B: 1837; D: 1910.
- BOOTH, J.H.; B: 1862; D: 1-22-1891.
- BOOTH, William N.; B: 1860; D: 1909.
- BOWEN, Brice B.; B: 1844; D: 1925; Ψ Civil War.
- BOWLEY, Louisa; B: 1810; D: May 1882.
- BOWLIN, Anna H. Seaton; B: 1870; D: 4-14-1909; w/o F.M.
- BOWLIN, Franklin M.; B: 1855; D: 1-10-1931.
- BOWLIN, Reppa L.; B: 1855; D: 9-4-1892; w/o F.M.
- BOYSEN, Andrew; B: 1864; D: 1922.
- BOYSEN, Christine; B: 1872; D: 1938.
- BOYSEN, John; B: 1879; D: 1937.
- BRAZIE, Fred E.; B: 1883; D: 1939.
- BRAZIE, Jay; B: 1854; D: 2-23-1902.
- BRAZIE, Raymond; (no dates).
- BREWSTER, Glen G.; D: 4-12-1935.
- BREWSTER, L.H. (or S.H.); (no dates).
- BRIDGEMAN, D.G.; B: 1812; D: 12-20-1872.
- BRIDGEMAN, M.D.; B: 1852; D: 4-3-1880.
- BROCKER, Mary Hulsebus; B: 1884; D: 1921.
- BROCKMAN, Ferdinand; B: 1862; D: 1926.
- BRODERSEN, Gena; B: 1843; D: 3-2-1910.
- BRODERSEN, Jacob; B: 1840; D: 12-2-1924.
- BROWN, Adam; B: 1865; D: 1-11-1937.
- BROWN, M.A.; B: 1850; D: 1925.
- BROWN, Rachel; B: 1848; D: 1920.
- BUCHER, --; [no dates].
- BUCK, Laura J.; B: 1866; D: 1907.

- BUCK, Louis J.; B: 1886; D: 1938.
- BUCK, Roscoe A.; B: 5-19-1888; D: 6-16-1931.
- BUCKMAN, A.W.; B: 1838; D: 5-27-1916.
- BUCKMAN, Annie D.; B: 1851; D: 9-29-1913; w/o John G.
- BUCKMAN, Emma V. (Hurst); B: 1839; D: 5-8-1882; w/o [Aaron N.]
- BUCKMAN, John C.; B: 1846; D: 7-25-1909, Newton, Ia.; h/o Annie D. Daniels.
- BURCHAM, Jane; B: 1844; D: 1935.
- BURCHAM, John; B: 1838; D: 1934.
- BURK, Dorinda; B: 1819; D: 9-7-1888; w/o H.S.
- BURK, Henry S., "Father"; B: 1818; D: 1-21-1899.
- BURR, R.E.; B: 1841; D: 7-28-1887; Ψ Co.I 28th Wis. Inf.
- BURROUGHS, Lloyd E.; B: 1-13-1908; D: 3-17-1928.
- BUSS, Albert; B: 1868; D: 3-15-1932; Ψ Co. E 43rd Wis. Inf.
- BUSS, Charley; B: 1857; D: 1933.
- BUTTS, Elizabeth; B: 1837; D: 1919; w/o W.B.
- BUTTS, Fred H. B: 1879; D: 1925.
- BUTTS, Wesley B; B: 1847; D: 1916.
- BYERS, Alexander; B: 1822; D: 6-14-1879; Ψ Mexican & Civil Wars.
- BYERS, Francis Ellsworth; B: 1886; D: 1905.
- BYERS, Howard Webster; B: 1856; D: 1928.
- CALDWELL, Charlie; D: 1-27-1940.
- CALDWELL, Joseph W.; B: 1869; D: 5-6-1869.
- CALDWELL, Lucinda; B: 1841; D: 12-18-1892.
- CALDWELL, T.C.; B: 6-23-1837; D: 6-25-1911.
- CALL, Margaret E. Lewis; B: 1879; D: 1931.
- CAMERY, Belle N.; B: 1874; D: 1938.
- CAMERY, Morgan A.; B: 1865; D: 1931.
- CAMPBELL, Fannie.; B: 1866; D: 3-30-1885.
- CAMPBELL, M. K.; B: 1837; D: 1928.
- CAMPBELL, Mamie E.; B: 1870; D: 3-30-1905.
- CAMPBELL, Mamie F., "Mother"; B: 1870; D: 1905.
- CAMPBELL, Mary E.; B: 1844; D: 2-13-1882.
- CAMPBELL, Owen E.; B: 1892; D: 1926.
- CAMPBELL, William Colin; B: 1855, Australia; D: 4-6-1924; h/o Emma F. Straight.
- CARL, A. C.; B: 1857; D: 1936.

- CARL, O. R.; B: 1869; D: 1938.
- CARL, W. H.; B: 1849; D: 1924.
- CARLSON, Carl J.; B: 1887; D: 1923.
- CARLSON, Margaret E.; B: 1872; D: 1920.
- CARLYLE, Adam; B: 1867; D: 1928.
- CARLYLE, Thomas R.; B: 1893; D: 1912.
- CARMICHAEL, Donald L.; B: 1897; D: 1935.
- CARMICHAEL, Douglas J.; B: 1872; D: 1938.
- CARMICHAEL, Neil; B: 1840; D: 11-21-1885.
- CARMICHAEL, Sanna; B: 1875; D: 7-26-1895.
- CARSON, Elizabeth; B: 1820; D: 5-25-1890.
- CARSTENSEN, Anna M.; B: 1892; D: 1938.
- CASEY, William; B: 1852; D: 1929.
- CASEY, James; B: 1829; D: 1908.
- CASEY, Mary; B: 1828; D: 1-23-1889; w/o James.
- CATIMEC, Charles; D: 2-10-1940.
- CHASE, Oliver T.; B: 1815; D: 3-24-1882.
- CHATBURN, Chas. D.; Age 1 yr.; s/o T.W.
- CHATBURN, Fred; (no dates).
- CHATBURN, Jonas W.; B: 1821; D: 1902.
- CHATBURN, Mary A.; (no dates).
- CHATBURN, Mary B.; B: 1821; D: 1900; w/o J.W.
- CHICHESTER, Eliphalet; B: 1804; D: 7-28-1877.
- CHRISTANSEN, Masinus; B: 1858; B: 7-21-1935.
- CHRISTENSEN, [Johanna] P.; B: 1847; D: 11-22-1913; w/o C.
- CHRISTENSEN, Adeline; B: 1924; D: 1928.
- CHRISTENSEN, Amelia; B: 1851; D: 1921; w/o L.C.
- CHRISTENSEN, Amy Smith; B: 1893; D: 1927; w/o Carl.
- CHRISTENSEN, Anders; B: 1892; D: 7-20-1912.
- CHRISTENSEN, Anna J.; B: 1869; D: 1934.
- CHRISTENSEN, Anna; B: 1889; D: 1921; w/o J.C.
- CHRISTENSEN, C. Anton; B: 1860; D: 2-26-1934.
- CHRISTENSEN, Carl; B: 1836; D: 1918.
- CHRISTENSEN, Christ J.; B: 1860; D: 1940.
- CHRISTENSEN, Christen; B: 1846; D: 12-4-1923.
- CHRISTENSEN, Ella; B: 1878; D: 1931.

- CHRISTENSEN, Eugene C.; D: 8-5-1939.
- CHRISTENSEN, Fern Daws; B: 1888; D: 1917; w/o J.C.
- CHRISTENSEN, Florence; B: 5-4-1896; D: 3-9-1917
- CHRISTENSEN, Gertrude M.; B: 1858; D: 1919.
- CHRISTENSEN, Grace A.; B: 1892; D: 1922; w/o Andrew W.
- CHRISTENSEN, Herb; D: 12-26-1939.
- CHRISTENSEN, J.C.; B: 1884; D: 1927.
- CHRISTENSEN, Jacob; (no dates).
- CHRISTENSEN, Jerry; (no dates).
- CHRISTENSEN, John; B: 1896; D: 1927; Ψ World War.
- CHRISTENSEN, Kathryn; B: 1890; D: 1927.
- CHRISTENSEN, Marilyn; D: May 1936.
- CHRISTENSEN, Marius; D: June 1919.
- CHRISTENSEN, Mike; B: 1872; D: 11-30-1931.
- CHRISTENSEN, Olive; B: 1869; D: 9-9-1935.
- CHRISTENSEN, Peter; B: 1865; D: 1906.
- CHRISTENSEN, Ralph; B: 1900; D: 1926.
- CHRISTENSEN, Rudolf Ener; B: 1908; D: 6-2-1929.
- CHRISTENSESN, Christian M.; B: 1853; D: 11-11-1904.
- CHRISTIANSEN, Anna Kasby; B: 1855; D: 1922; w/o Marinus.
- CHRISTIE, Ann, "Mother"; B: 1824; D: 7-15-1900.
- CLAUSEN, Maren; B: 1835; D: 1-4-1900; w/o J.
- CLAUSSEN, Jorgen; B: 1838; D: 1903.
- CLAYTON, Samuel B.; B: 1891; D: 1918.
- CLEMENSON, Christine; B: 1860; D: 11-20-1937.
- CLEVELAND, Luella Noble; B: 1861; D: 1924.
- CLEVELAND, Wm. F.; B: 1845, New York, N.Y.; D: 2-19-1916; Ψ Co.M 2nd Ia. Cav.
- CLOSSON, Aaron; B: 1815; D: 12-19-1897; Ψ Co.I 32nd O.
- CLOSSON, Warren; B: 1834; D: 8-15-1904; Ψ 142nd Ind. Inf.
- COBB, Elliott A.; B: 1843; D: 1-12-1925; Ψ Co. A 55th O.
- COBB, Fanny; (no dates).
- COBB, Fern; (no dates).
- COBB, G.C.; (no dates).
- COBB, George Floyd; (no dates).
- COBB, Nettie; B: 1856; D: 3-24-1935.
- COBB, Omar; (no dates).

- COCKERELL, William Hoburn; B: 1852; D: 1895.
- COCKERELL, William Walter; B: 1879; D: 1904.
- COCKERELL; Elenor McMillan; B: 1849; D: 1906.
- COENON, John, "Father"; B: 1830; D: 2-9-1906.
- COENON, Margaret; D: 10-4-1839.
- COLBURN, Harriet R.; B: 1851; D: 1931.
- COLBURN, M. M.; B: 1926 [1826]; D: 1878.
- COLEMAN, M.H.; B: 1813; D: 12-21-1881; Ψ GAR marker.
- COLNER, Mary D. (Weber); B: 1836; D: 9-4-1884; w/o John Colner.
- CONLIN, Martha C.; B: 1882; D: 1933; Ψ World War Eur[ope?].
- CONRAD, Toy; B: 1894; D: 1934; w/o Arthur.
- COOK, Almon Moss; B: 1863; D: 4-13-1900.
- COOK, Elihu L. (Dr.); B: 1839; D: 3-28-1916; Ψ Civil War.
- COOK, H. M., "Father"; B: 1844; D: 1912.
- COOK, Harry; (no dates).
- COOK, John L.; B: 4-29-1893; D: 1920.
- COOK, Mary E.; B: 1839; D: 2-26-1931; w/o E.L.
- COOK, Stella; B: 1874; D: 1930.
- COOPER, Laura Walters; B: 1862; D: 1-17-1937.
- COPELAND, Dwight; B: 11-15-1890; D: 7-26-1930.
- COPELAND, Elizabeth Ann; B: 1856; D: 1935; w/o Scott.
- COPELAND, Scott; B: 1852; D: 1934.
- CORWIN, Kezia M.; B: 1814 D: 1887.
- COX, Elder J.M.; B: 1823; D: 9-9-1910.
- COX, Elma L.; B: 1897; D: 1917; w/o L.
- COX, George W.; B: 1859; D: 1932.
- COX, Julia A.; B: 1870; D: 1909; w/o Jno. M.
- COX, Mary; B: 1825; D: 1-18-1898; w/o J.M.
- COX, Sarah; B: 1834; D: 4-2-1906.
- CRANDALL, Achsan; B: 1811; D: 3-19-1865.
- CRUZAN, J.C. (Dr.); B: 1817; D: 5-10-1899.
- CRUZAN, Minerva T.F.; B: 1825; D: 1910.
- CULLISON, George W.; B: 1848; D: 1923.
- #CULLISON, Jennie Gates; B: 1849 D: 11-16-18[98]; w/o G.W.
- CULLISON, Shelby M.; B: 1887, Harlan; D: 1-18-1925.
- CUPPY, Darcus C.; B: 1839; D: 1914.
- CURRIER, Carlton; B: 1868; D: 2-23-1899.

- CURTIS, Maryle Edwards; B: 1883; D: 2-8-1913.
- CURTIS, William; B: 1852; D: 11-1-1885.
- CURTISS, Charles A.; [no dates].
- CUSTER, Arthur; B: 1860, near Harlan; D: 5-26-1932; Omaha Journal-Herald, 7-9-32.
- CUSTER, Catherine; B: 1846; D: 1936; w/o Henry.
- CUSTER, Emma; B: 1863; D: 1935.
- CUSTER, Henry; B: 1844; D: 1926; Ψ GAR Marker.
- CUSTER, Lola A. Rodgers; B: 11-24-1881; D: 12-1-1917.
- DAHLOF, Helmfred B.; B: 1856; D: 1931.
- DALES, David G.; B: 1856; D: 1939; Ψ Spanish-American War.
- DALES, M[a]e E.; B: 1871; D: 1939.
- DALEY, Daniel; B: 1840, West Stockbridge, MA; D: 1-27-1907; h/o Jennie Grant.
- DALLING, Bonetti; D: 6-8-1932.
- DANGAARD, "Father"; B: 1860; D: 1933.
- DANGAARD, Christen C.; B: 1861; D: 4-14-1908.
- DAVIS, Charles M.; B: 1855; D: 1920.
- DAVIS, Edward W.; B: 1839, Conn.; D: 9-17-1903; h/o May Benham.
- DAVIS, Esther M.; B: 1905; D: 1927.
- DAVIS, James E.; B: 1848; D: 12-13-1928.
- DAVIS, Josephine E.; B: 1851; D: 11-30-1936.
- DAVIS, Leah Kinney; B: 1812; D: 1900.
- DAVIS, Mary Benham; B: 1855; D: 3-4-1934; w/o Edw. W.
- DAVIS, Sarah C.; B: 1845; D: 4-29-1880.
- DAVIS, William John; B: 1838; D: 1-16-1924; Ψ Civil War.
- DAVIS, William; B: 1856; D: 1938.
- DAWSON, Mariam; B: 1861; D: 9-27-1893; d/o S.S. Barter.
- DAYTON, Irwin O.; B: 1874; D: Feb 1894.
- DAYTON, Shailor H.; B: 1831; D: Mar 1894.
- DAYTON, Tabitha; B: 1849; D: Dec 1931.
- DAYTON, Verner L.; B: 1870; D: Jun 1924.
- DEEN, Clarence H.; B: 1891; D: 1920.
- DEEN, Emma, "Mother"; B: 1852; D: 1931.
- DEEN, Flora A.; B: 1873; D: 1914.
- DEEN, J. H.; B: 1864; D: 1926.

- DeFORD, John R.; B: 1851; D: 1916.
- DeSILVA, J. W.; B: 1834; D: 3-21-1890.
- DeSILVA, Lydia J. (Striker); B: 1844; D: 1921.
- DEWEY, Chester; B: 1833; D: 12-26-1899.
- DEWEY, Nancy J.; B: 1845; D: 9-7-1931; w/o Chester.
- DEWEY, Samantha C.; D: 7-20-1865; Age 49.
- DEWEY, William A.; B: 1864; D: 3-3-1912.
- DICKMAN, Elma W.; B: 1871; D: 3-16-1914.
- DICKMAN, N. M.; B: 1838; D: 3-4-1875; Ψ Civil War.
- DINESEN, Petrina (Nielsen); B: 1882; D: 12-1-1922; w/o J.S.
- DONAHUE, Matilda, "Mother"; B: 1854; D: 1929.
- DONAHUE, Oscar S.; B: 1857; D: 1931.
- DONNAN, Grace L.; B: 1877; D: 9-19-1935.
- DONNAN, H.; B: 1866; D: 12-24-1925.
- DOUGLAS, M.T.J.; B: 1840; D: 12-24-1880.
- DOWNES, W.O.; B: 1845; D: 3-19-1874; Ψ Co.C 33rd Ia. Inf.
- DOWNEY, Cyrus K.; B: 1845; D: 1-20-1919.
- DOWNEY, Margaret E.; B: 1840; D: 11-9-1912; w/o C.M.
- DRAKE, C.L.; B: 1843; D: 9-23-1910; Ψ Co.I 12th Ill. Inf.
- DRAKE, Matilda F.; B: 1846; D: 3-23-1909; Age 63; w/o C.L.
- DUKE, Elizabeth G.; B: 1844; D: 9-10-1905; w/o Thos.
- DUKE, Mabel E.; B: 1885; D: 4-8-1939; w/o Thos.
- DUKE, Thomas Lynn; B: 1903; D: 1-14-1935.
- DUKE, Thomas, "Father"; B: 1849; D: 10-2-1919.
- DUNLAVY, James D.; B: 1858; D: 11-18-1929.
- DUNLAVY, Jennie E.; B: 1859; D: 5-9-1936.
- DUNNINGTON, Asa; B: 1886; D: 1927.
- DUNNINGTON, James F.; B: 1841; D: 1922; Ψ Civil War.
- DUNNINGTON, Mildred; B: 1871; D: 3-7-1904.
- DUNNINGTON, Rebecca A.; B: 1851; D: 1938; w/o James F.
- EIGLER, Irene V.; B: 6-11-1902; D-1-5-1935.
- ELLIS, Viola Fay; D: 6-11-1938.
- EOKARS, George; B: 1838; D: 1908.
- EOKARS, Julia Piper; B: 1841; D: 1920.
- ERICKSON, Carrie, "Mother"; B: 1852; D: 1921.
- ERICKSON, E. H.; B: 1854; D: 1923.
- ERICKSON, Edward T.; B: 1893; D: 1920; Ψ World War.

- ERICKSON, Enoch; B: 1841; D: 1923.
- ERICKSON, Mathilde; B: 1862; D: 1932.
- ERIKSEN, Erik; B: 1877; D: 12-14-1918.
- ERRETT, F.T.; B: 1849; D: 1938.
- ERRETT, George; B: 1815; D: 10-9-1894.
- ERRETT, Nevada; B: 1852; D: 7-24-1899; ψ G[A]R Marker.
- ERRETT, Susan; B: 1810; D: 2-12-1900; w/o J.
- ERRETT, William H.; B: 1843; D: 8-16-1923; Ψ Co.T 126th [Ill. Inf.]
- ESCHER, Charles E. Jr.; B: 1872; D: 8-10-1925.
- ESCHER, Charles Sr.; B: 1840, Germany; D: 3-16-1918.
- ESCHER, Edwin F.; B: 1863; D: 1923.
- ESCHER, Henry Anson; B: 1851; D: 7-21-1930; h/o Romancey.
- ESCHER, Herbert E.; B: 1888; D: 1933.
- ESCHER, Louisa K.; B: 1840; D: 1-17-1884.
- ESCHER, Minnie Louise; B: 1882; D: 7-8-1922; w/o Wilson A. Butke [Bertke].
- ESCHER, Romancey Grauel; B: 1855; D: 12-29-1927; w/o Henry Anson.
- EVANS, George; B: 1857; D: 1930.
- FAIRFIELD, Mary B.; B: 1827; D: 6-1878.
- FAIRFIELD, William B.; B: 1827; D: Dec 1893.
- FALL, G. W.; B: 1823; D: 3-11-1890.
- FARROW, Esther; B: 1886; D: 1907.
- FARROW, Francis A.; B: 1821; D: 1905.
- FERGUSON, Charles; B: 1888; D: 1908.
- FERGUSON, Mary E.; B: 1851; D: 1914.
- FERGUSON, Ruben C.; B: 1856; D: 1920.
- FERRY, Mawin L. (male); B: 1909; D: 8-8-1935.
- #FINDLEY, Aneta; Wife of Merle Findley – See HARRIS-FINDLEY, Aneta [Entry written between typed lines].
- FINDLEY, Louisa S., "Mother"; B: 1857; D: 9-23-1930.
- FIREBAUGH, Lucy; B: 1864; D: 4-5-1910.
- FISCUS, C.O.; (no dates).
- FISCUS, E.; (no dates).
- FISCUS, R.S.; (no dates).
- FISH, Anna M.; B: 1849; D: 1927.

- FISH, Edward F.; B: 1835; D: 1933; Ψ GAR marker.
- FISHER, Azariah; B: 1827; D: 4-20-1874.
- FISHER, Gideon; B: 1852; D: 1-19-1916.
- FISHER, Iva Gertrude; B: 1876; D: 7-11-1908; w/o Earl.
- #FISHER, Rose E. (Ross); (All under ROSS, Rose E.).
- FISHER, Ruth M.; B: 1908; D: 1933.
- FISHER, Sarah Ellen; B: 1854; D: 3-17-1935; w/o Gideon.
- FLAGLER, Geo. G.; B: 1821; D: 3-30-1899.
- FLAUGH, Ellen M.; B: 1873; D: 1938.
- FORREST, Amanda; B: 1827; D: 2-17-1886; w/o J. Forrist [Forrest].
- FORREST, Charles; B: 1861; D: 5-14-1885.
- FORREST, James; B: 1826; D: 2-19-1892.
- FOSS, Robert P.; B: 1834; D: 7-29-1901.
- FRANKLIN, Thomas A.; B: 1864; D: 1924.
- FRAZIER, Mable (Perry); B: 1876; D: 1923; w/o Fred.
- FREDRICKSEN, --, "Father & Mother"; B: 1836; D: 1918.
- FREDRICKSEN, Anna; B: 1843; D: 9-15-1908.
- FREDRICKSEN, Christian; B: 1874; D: 5-28-1912.
- FREDRICKSEN, Emil; B: 1882; D: 1919.
- FREDRICKSEN, Etta Mae; B: 3-17-1891; D: 12-3-1918.
- FREDRICKSEN, Lars; B: 1842; D: 2-10-1928.
- FREDRICKSEN, Louis C.; B: 1899; D: 1918; Ψ World War.
- FRENCH, Jason C.; B: 1838; D: 2-22-1891.
- FROST, --; B: 1856; D: 8-13-1897.
- FROST, Dr. L.D.; B: 1834; D: 2-14-1904.
- FROST, Estella Taylor; D: 4-7-1906; Age 29; w/o C.C.
- FROTZ, Elizabeth; B: 1832; D: 2-20-1899.
- FROTZ, Menzo; B: 1858; D: 9-21-1934.
- FROYD, Carl Stanly; (no dates).
- FULLER, C. Elmer; B: 1875; D: 1936.
- FULLER, Charles C.; B: 1850; D: 1-13-1914.
- FULLER, Eunice; B: 1852; D: 1-26-1924; w/o Chas. C.
- GALBREATH, John B.; B: 1847; D: 7-11-1912; Ψ Civil War.
- GALBREATH, Malissa; B: 1856; D: 6-15-1933.
- GANSER, Daniel Z.; B: 1853; D: 5-19-1923.
- GANSER, John Alphur; B: 1876; D: 9-18-1898; Ψ Co.C 51st Ia.

- GANSER, S. Earl; B: 1879; D: 1922.
- GARDNER, Cora A.; B: 1900; D: 1933.
- GARDNER, Peter H.; B: 1863; D: 1933.
- GARLICK, Herman; B: 1858; D: 4-11-1907.
- GARLICK, Susan A.; B: 1857; D: 1919.
- GARST, Ira D.; B: 1858; D: 9-20-1936.
- GARST, Ira; (no dates).
- GATES, Jennie; B: 1849; D: 11-16-1898; w/o G.W. Cullison.
- GEARHART, Frank; D: 3-29-1940.
- GEARHART, Hoyt Ellie; B: 1916; D: 1935.
- GEORGE, Agnes; B: 1849; D: 6-22-1898.
- GEORGE, Elizabeth; B: 1824; D: 6-16-1882.
- GIBBS, Alon[s]o C.; B: 1836; D: 4-12-1915.
- GIBBS, Elizabeth; B: 1825; D: 1-26-1890.
- GIBBS, Ella Florence; B: 1858; D: 1916; w/o For[es]t.
- GIBBS, Forest; B: 1855; D: 1924.
- GIBBS, George Sabin; B: 1848; D: 7-8-1901.
- GIBBS, Orren A.; B: 1814; D: 9-12-1887.
- GIBBS, Winfred R.; B: 1846; D: 1-12-1910.
- GIBFORD, Russel; (no dates).
- GILLESPIE, Frederick M.; B: 1841; D: 3-1-1901.
- GILLESPIE, Mary E.; B: 1843; D: 2-13-1923.
- GILLETTE, Everette; B: 1896; D: 1918; Ψ World War.
- GILLETTE, George T.; B: 1871; D: 1935.
- GILLETTE, Hazel V.; B: 1894; D: 1918.
- GILLETTE, John T.; B: 1842; D: 7-11-1917.
- GILLETTE, Margaret E.; B: 1838; D: 2-27-1917.
- GILLETTE, Sarah F.; B: 1849; D: 2-5-1913.
- GILLETTE, William H.; B: 1835; D: 1-18-1911.
- GILMORE, James P., "Father"; B: 1842; D: 1921; Ψ GAR marker.
- GILMORE, Margaret H.; B: 1839; D: 1923.
- GINGERY, George E.; B: 1876; D: 7-16-1906; s/o Lewis.
- GINGERY, Lewis; B: 1847; D: 5-19-1895.
- GINGERY, Lewis; B: 1876; D: 7-16-1906; s/o Lewis.
- GISH, "Father"; (no dates).
- GISH, "Mother"; (no dates).
- GISH, Colda; (no dates).

- GISH, Eugene; (no dates).
- GISH, Ruthe; (no dates).
- GODDARD, Leon E.; B: 1898; D: 1918; Ψ World War.
- GODDARD, Martha J.; B: 1845; D: 7-16-1910.
- GOFF, J.S.; (no dates); Ψ Co.D WV Cav.
- GOODIN (GOODEN), John; B: 1822; D: 5-9-1890; Ψ GAR marker.
- GOODING, Fred; B: 1838; D: 1914; Ψ Civil War.
- GOODING, Matilda; B: 1845; D: 1930.
- GOODMAN, Martha; B: 1823; D: 7-17-1889; w/o J.
- GOODNER, Dale O.; B: 1890; D: 1939.
- GOODNER, Edith J.; B: 1824; D: 5-26-1902.
- GOODNER, Fannie, "Mother"; B: 1865; D: 1928.
- GOODNER, Frances N.; B: 1894; D: 1939.
- GOODNER, W.D.; B: 1820; D: 7-31-1898.
- GOODNER, William, "Father"; B: 1864; D: 1934.
- GOODYEAR, Barbara Wyland; B: 1840; D: 11-29-1919.
- GOODYEAR, Christian; B: 1829; D: 3-10-1874.
- GOULD, Ada R.; B: 1882; D: 1934; w/o John.
- GOULD, John P.; B: 1877; D: 1935.
- GRABILL, --; D: 1-20-1940; w/o John.
- GRABILL, Anna C.; B: 1850; D: 1937.
- GRABILL, Ira, "Father"; B: 1839; D: 1922; Ψ Civil War.
- GRAF, Charles; B: 1856; D: 10-10-1934.
- GRAF, Mary A.; B: 1857; D: 9-6-1928.
- GRAUEL, C.D.; B: 1859; D: 1925.
- GRAUEL, Etta E.; B: 1865; D: 1930; m/o C.D.
- GRAUEL, Romancy; B: 1855; D: 12-29-1927; w/o Henry A. Escher.
- GRAVES, --; (no dates); w/o O.F.
- GRAVES, Carrie Daws; B: 1856; D: 4-2-1912.
- GRAVES, Celina; B: 1848; D: 1927; w/o C.E.
- GRAVES, Charles Elliott; B: 1905; D: 1928.
- GRAVES, Charles; B: 1852; D: 2-10-1916.
- GRAVES, Cyrus E.; B: 1849; D: 5-24-1932.
- GRAVES, Ella; B: 1821; D: 8-3-1908; w/o [G]uy W.
- GRAVES, John; D: 7-16-1939.
- GRAVES, Margaret Jessie; B: 4-16-1912; D: 2-2-1934.
- GRAVES, Mary Fairfield; B: 1848; D: 9-7-1924; w/o Horace.

- GRAVES, Rodney E.; B: 1872; D: 6-28-1916.
- GRAVES. Horace; B: 1843; D: 4-17-1899.
- GRAY, Nicholas; B: 1851; D: 5-23-1906.
- GRAY, Roys S.; B: 1895; D: 1924.
- GREGORY, James D.; B: 1859; D: 1939.
- GREGORY, Mary B.; B: 1832; D: 1916.
- GRIES, Henry, "Father"; B: 1857; D: 1927.
- GRIES, Pauline; B: 1862; D: 1924; w/o Henry.
- GRIFFIN, Lilly G. [Emily?]; B: 1834; D: 6-13-1913; w/o W.H.
- GRIFFIN, W.H.; B: 1827; D: 6-12-1891.
- #GRIFFITH, Benj. [B.]; B: 1823; D: 1901; h/o Hannah Lash; Ψ GAR marker.
- #GRIFFITH, Benj. B. Jr.; B: 1861; D: 1923; h/o Mary A. Collier.
- GRIFFITH, Hannah M. (Lash); B: 1831; D: 1901; w/o B.B.
- GRIFFITH, Hiram F.; B: 1861; D: 4-12-1904.
- GRIFFITH, Mary A. (Collier); B: 1865; D: 1885; w/o Benj. B. Jr.
- HACK, Christian; B: 1834; D: 11-14-1911; Ψ Co.A 29th Ia. Inf.
- HACK, H.P.; B: 1853; D: 1926.
- HACK, Lytha A.; B: 1844; D: 1918; w/o Christian.
- HACK, Ole S.; B: 1874; D: 1913.
- HAMBLIN, Floyd C.; B: 4-25-1898; D: 11-1-1914.
- HAMBLIN, Hannah; B: 1843; D: 1928; w/o J.W.
- HAMBLIN, James W.; B: 1840; D: 1930.
- HAMMER, Otto R.; B: 1871; D: 1929.
- HAMMES, Jacob; B: 1856; D: 1926.
- HANSEN, Alfred; B: 1880; D: Mar 1912.
- HANSEN, Bina A.; B: 1886; D: 7-4-1910; w/o Earl.
- HANSEN, Chris J.; B: 1871; D: 9-1-1930.
- HANSEN, Claus, "Father"; B: 1865; D: 1934.
- HANSEN, Hans A.; B: 1849; D: 1938.
- HANSEN, Jennie; (no dates).
- HANSEN, Jens H.; B: 1855; D: 5-21-1885.
- HANSEN, Knud; B: 1868; D: 11-28-1911; (wife also buried there).
- HANSEN, Mabel Grace; B: 1897; D: 1923; w/o Harry E.
- HANSEN, Maren; B: 1841; D: 8-17-1919.
- HANSEN, Maria; B: 1842; D: 8-10-1931; w/o Peter Carl.
- HANSEN, Marie; B: 10-10-1884; D: 2-8-1914; w/o Hans N.

- HANSEN, Marie; B: 1836; D: 1915; w/o P.C.
- HANSEN, Marie; B: 1836; D: 1915; w/o Peter C.
- HANSEN, Nis E.; B: 1883; D: 1937.
- HANSEN, Peter C.; B: 1832; D: 1903.
- #HANSEN, Simon Carl; B: 1885; D: 1938.
- HANSEN, Truels; B: 1841; D: 4-11-1913.
- HANSEN; Myers; B: 1872; D: 7-24-1910.
- HANSON, I.M.; B: 1882; D: 1935.
- HANSON, Nels C.; B: 1841; D: 1920.
- HANSON, Ole; B: 1814; D: 1888.
- HARDMAN, "Mother"; (no dates).
- HARRIS, Elvina K.; B: 1887; D: 1918.
- HARRIS, Julia D.; B: 1890; D: 1939.
- HARRIS, Lyman; (no dates).
- HARRIS-FINDLEY, Aneta Gale; B: 1913; D: 1932; w/o Merel Findley.
- HARVEY, J.; B: 1829; D: 8-6-1882.
- HARVEY, Lucy Ann; B: 1824; D: 12-1-1902; w/o J.H.
- HASKINS, Almira; B: 1872; D: 1936.
- HASKINS, Joel; B: 1835; D: 9-29-1906.
- HASKINS, Nancy J.; B: 1845; D: 5-1-1928.
- HASKINS, Oran; (no dates).
- HAUN, Ida; B: 1870; D: 1924.
- HAVICK, A.A., "Father"; B: 1848; D: 1938.
- HAVICK, Adelia, "Mother"; B: 1856; D: 1926.
- HAYWARD, Annie Pearl; B: 1877; D: 7-26-1913.
- HEFLIN, Hulda M.; B: 1883; D: 12-29-1930.
- HEFLIN, Lucy; B: 1847; D: 1930; w/o S.G.
- HEFLIN, S.G.; B: 1845; D: 4-23-1910; Ψ Co.B 102nd Ill. Inf.
- HEILESEN, Tillie, "Mother"; B: 1868; D: 1925.
- HEINTZ, Elizabeth; B: 1859; D: 3-10-1923; w/o P.
- HEINTZ, Nicholas; B: 1821; D: 11-17-1903.
- HENDERSON, Mary; B: 1841; D: 2-6-1897; w/o Samuel.
- HENDERSON, Samuel; B: 1845; D: 7-22-1909; Ψ Civil War.
- HENDERSON, Shadrack; D: Apr 22, 1910; Ψ Co.A 11th Ia. Inf.
- HENDRICHSEN, Alice; B: 1892; D: 1928.
- HENRICHS, E.W.; D: 8-18-1938.

- HERTERT, Emil Mathias; B: 1854; D: 1923.
- HERTERT, John P.; D: 8-24-1936.
- HERTERT, John P.; D: 8-24-1936; Harlan (res & burial).
- HERVEY, Samuel C.; B: 1848; D: 1934.
- HESS, Christian; B: 1851; D: 1921.
- HESS, Eliza Ann; B: 1855; D: 1935.
- HESS, Mary Jacobsen; B: 1881; D: 3-19-1932.
- HESS, Nicholas; B: 1853; D: 6-28-1833; (his wife buried there also).
- HESS-HANSEN, Magreta; B: 1865; D: 5-21-1933.
- HETZEL, John; B: 1851, Va.; D: 9-17-1918.
- HILL, F.J.; (no dates); Ψ Civil War.
- HILLIE, Sarah J.; B: 1835; D: 12-11-1888.
- HILLYER, Nathaniel T.; B: 1846, Caldwell, Noble Co. O.; D: -- (res. Harlan); s/o Wm. & Kate Cain Hillyer; (Guthrie Co. history 1907).
- HOISINGTON, George A.; B: 1858; D: 12-5-1928.
- HOLDSWORTH, Jane; B: 1829; D: 8-25-1907.
- HOLLAR, Elizabeth; B: 1808; D: 1892.
- HOLMES, Amanda; B: 1856; D: 11-20-1904.
- HOLMES, C.W.; B: 1849; D: 11-19-1915.
- HOLMES, Ella Walters; B: 1864; D: 1904.
- HOLMES, Laura Emily; B: 1892; D: 1913.
- HOLMES, Laura; B: 1892; D: 1913.
- HOLMES, William; B: 1879; D: 1924.
- HOOVER, Eli E.; B: 1848; D: 5-25-1918.
- HOOVER, Martha; B: 1849; D: 3-25-1927.
- HOOVER, Walter J.; B: 1885; D: 6-13-1915.
- #HOSKINS, Celia E.; B: 6-16-1897; D: May 1927; d/o Charles & Eva Oakes Caldwell; 2nd w/o Elmer LeRoy Hoskins; info from Beulah Hoskins Woodin, d/o E.L. & Celia Hoskins.
- HOSKINS, Charles A.; B: 1884; D: 9-9-1912; s/o E.J. & S.L.
- HOSKINS, Eli J., "Father"; B: 1850; D: 12-15-1923.
- HOSKINS, Ethel F.; B: 1-4-1896; D: 11-21-1915; w/o Leroy.
- HOSKINS, Sarah K., "Mother"; B: 1855; D: 1-23-1937.
- HOTCHKISS, Anne E. Shepherd; B: 1869; D: 1926; w/o Louis J.
- HOWARD, Nelson L.; B: 1846; D: 1887; Ψ Civil War.
- HOWARTH, Geo. Fred; B: 1893; D: 1925; Ψ World War.

- HOWLETTE, Ruth E.; B: 1836; D: 1916.
- HOYT, S.J. (Dr.); B: 1839; D: 5-5-1909; Ψ Co.I 4th Ia. Inf.
- HUBER, Fritz; B: 1885; D: 6-16-1887.
- HUBER, John; B: 1853; D: 9-10-1931.
- HUBER, Mary K.; B: 1866; D: 6-30-1938.
- HUFFMAN, John H.; B: 1839; D: 3-9-1930; Ψ Co.F 31 Ind. Inf.
- HUGH[E]S, Nancy; B: 1826; D: 1 Feb 1899.
- HULSEBUS, Chas. Edwin; B: 6-23-1892; D: 7-29-1929; Ψ World War.
- HULSEBUS, Harm; B: 1842; D: 1922.
- HULSEBUS, Johanna; B: 1859; D: 1930.
- HUNT, Mary E.; B: 1833; D: 10-27-1907; w/o John B.
- HUNT, Mary F.; B: 1851; D: 5-24-1931.
- HUNT, Pardon B.; B: 1842; D: 5-6-1894.
- HUNT, Seth; B: 1816; D: 6-5-1891.
- HURD, Elmer; B: 1887; D: 1918.
- HURLESS, Catherine; B: 1832; D: 5-8-1898; w/o S.F.
- HURLESS, S.F.; B: 1823; D: 5-23-1884.
- HURST, Emma V. Buckman; B: 1839; D: 5-28-1882; w/o A.M. Buckman.
- HURST, Malinda Harter; B: 1852; D: 6-25-1910.
- HYLER, Eddie; (no dates).
- HYLER, Mabel; (no dates).
- INGVERTSEN, Claus; B: 1862; D: 1884.
- INLOW, J.E.; B: 1846; D: Nov 1911.
- IWANS, Mrs.--; D: 1890.
- JACK, George Earl; B: 1873; D: 1936.
- JACK, Harriet L. (Lamb); D: 1913; w/o J.T.
- JACK, John Phillip; B: 1874; D: 1926.
- JACK, John T. (Col.); B: 1838, Pa.; D: 8-4-1912, Long Beach, Calif.; Ψ Civil War.
- JACOBSEN, --; (no dates); w/o Jens.
- JACOBSEN, Andrew, "Father"; B: 1860; D: 1928.
- JACOBSEN, Ann M., "Mother"; B: 1863; D: 1936.
- JACOBSEN, Mrs. --; (no dates).
- JACOBSEN, Peter; (no dates).
- JACOBSEN, Sena; B: 1857; D: 10-3-1930.

- JAMES, Florence C.; B: 1862; D: 1921; w/o Jno.
- JAMES, John; B: 1855; D: 1932.
- JAMES, Margaret; D: 1-27-1881; w/o O.C.
- JARVIS, Elihu; B: 1837; D: 1917.
- JARVIS, John N.; B: 1864; D: 1927.
- JARVIS, Lovina W.; B: 1838; D: 1922.
- JENKINS, Alice L.; B: 1873; D: 4-15-1880.
- JENSEN, Alfred J.; B: 12-14-1891, Denmark; D: 4-14-1934; h/o Myrtle Faurshou; Ψ World War.
- JENSEN, Andrew; B: 1885; D: 1927.
- JENSEN, Ane; B: 1844; D: 3-4-1893; w/o Loren.
- JENSEN, Anna E.; B: 1865; D: 1936.
- JENSEN, Carl; B: 1878; D: 1937.
- JENSEN, Chris P.; B: 1843; D: 1926.
- JENSEN, Ida; B: 1863; D: 1916; w/o A.P.
- JENSEN, Jens C.; B: 1876; D: 1928.
- JENSEN, Johanna M.; B: 1852; D: 1927.
- JENSEN, Julia M.; B: 1866; D: 1930.
- JENSEN, Loren C.; B: 1856; D: 1921.
- JENSEN, Mabel (Mrs.); D: 2-4-1940.
- JENSEN, Marcus C.; B: 1859; D: 1919.
- JENSEN, Marie; B: 1867; D: 1924; w/o Julius.
- JENSEN, Mary; D: 1-26-1883.
- JENSEN, Sina or Lina; B: 1865; D: 1919.
- JENSEN, Thomas; B: 1855; D: 1931; h/o Johanna.
- JEPSON, George; B: 1851; D: 4-10-1827.
- JERGENSEN, Elizabeth; (no dates).
- JESPERSEN, Anna K.; B: 1838; D: 5-22-1914; w/o Hans.
- JESPERSEN, Hans; B: 1843; D: 2-2-1910.
- JESPERSEN, Sarah Katring[a]; D: 11-6-1935.
- JESSEN, Agveta; (no dates).
- JOHNSON, --; (no dates); w/o James.
- JOHNSON, "Mother"; B: 1821; D: 4-2-1917.
- JOHNSON, Elmer A.; B: 1883; D: 2-23-1906.
- JOHNSON, Hannah; B: 1850; D: 5-22-1913; w/o Henry.
- JOHNSON, Hans; (no dates).
- JOHNSON, Henry, "Father"; B: 1853; D: 5-15-1892.

- JOHNSON, Isabelle; B: 1884; D: 1920.
- JOHNSON, James; (no dates).
- JOHNSON, Loren S.; B: 1847; D: 3-19-1932.
- JOHNSON, Margretha, "Mother"; B: 1845; D: 1932.
- JOHNSON, Matilda C.; B: 1848; D: 1-2-1913; w/o Loren.
- JOHNSON,Chris, "Father"; B: 1850, D: 1931.
- JORGENSEN, Johanna M.; B: 1863; D: 1932; w/o T.C.
- JOYCE, Wm. Patrick; B: 1890; D: 1923; h/o Mayne Allen; Ψ World War.
- JUHL, N.E.; B: 1864; D: 9-12-1935.
- JUHL, Sarah A.; B: 1854; D: 7-4-1914.
- JUSTESEN, Ane Magrate; B: 1820; D: 1903.
- JUSTICE, Gustavis A.; B: 1857; D: 1933.
- KAYS, Anna; B: 1853; D: 1935.
- KAYS, Anna; B: 1853; D: 1935.
- KAYS, Frank; B: 1847; D: 1930; Ψ Civil War.
- KAYS, Robert Huber; B: 1919; D: 1936.
- KEEP, Lois; B: 1838; D: 9-16-1917.
- KEEP, William R.; B: 1823; D: 6-27-1911; Ψ Mexican War.
- KEES, Clarence; (no dates).
- KEES, H.B., "Father"; B: 1835; D: 9-4-1930.
- KEES, Martha A., "Mother"; B: 1838; D: 1-13-1917.
- KEES, Sarah Jane; B: 1866; D: 2-17-1882.
- KELLER, C.E.; B: 1849; D: 11-19-1898.
- KELLEY, Charles E.; B: 6-15-1905; D: 6-20-1929.
- KELLEY, W.W.; B: 1860; D: 12-6-1936.
- KELLOGG, William P.; B: 1846; D: 1914; Ψ Civil War.
- KEMP, Anna W.; B: 1859; D: 9-25-1890.
- KEMP, C.P. or C/H. (Mrs.); B: 1859; D: 9-25-1898.
- KEMP, Clarence; B: 1858; D: 1924.
- KEMP, Lawrence; B: 1858; D: 7-12-1904.
- KENT, J.W.; B: 1859; D: 1935.
- KENT, James; (no dates).
- KENT, Karl K.; B: 1888; D: 1918.
- KENT, S.J.;B: 1859; D: 1926.
- KERR, Leonard; B: 1892; D: 1920.
- KERR, Louis M.; B: 1864; D: 1940.

- KEVAN, Clarence R.; B: 1872; D: 1926.
- KILCORN, --; B: 1839; D: 2-19-1908; w/o Patrick.
- KILCORN, "Brother"; B: 1899; D: 1920.
- KILCORN, Ellen; B: 1864; D: 1913.
- KILCORN, Katie; B: 1869; D: 1938.
- KILCORN, Margaret; B: 1866; D: 3-2-1909; w/o Thos. P.
- KILCORN, Patrick; B: 1828; D: 12-21-1904.
- KILCORN, Thomas P.; B: 1863; D: 9-29-1929.
- KING, Ulysses C.; B: 1865; D: 1922.
- KINSEY, B.I.; (no dates); h/o Lillie; Ψ Civil War.
- KINSEY, Charles; B: 1811; D: 9-6-1892.
- KINSEY, Charles; B: 1877; D: 7-4-1903.
- KINSEY, Elsa A.; B: 1857; D: 1925; m/o Chas.
- KINSEY, Homer L.; D: 1903.
- KINSEY, Lillie; B: 1852; D: 3-4-1889; w/o B.F. [B.I.]
- KINSEY, Louisa; B: 1837; D: 4-18-1905; w/o Newton.
- KINSEY, Mary; B: 1815; D: 3-12-1898; w/o Chas.
- KINSEY, Newton; B: 1835; D: 8-18-1918.
- KINSEY, Sarah; B: 1817; D: 3-24-1875.
- KINSEY. Guy Elwood; B: 1878; D: 3-5-1898.
- KIRBY, James; (no dates).
- KIRBY, William; B: 1849; D: 1889.
- KLITGARD, Agnes K.; B: 1895; D: 1920; w/o Andrew C.
- KNUDSEN, Ane; B: 1834; D: 3-25-1920.
- KNUDSEN, Rev. S.; B: 1832; D: 1-15-1915.
- KNUDSEN, Soren (Or Loren); B: 1857; D: 9-22-1915.
- KOCK, Wilhelm; B: 1867; D: 1921.
- KOEPKE, Tillis; B: 1880; D: 2-6-1913; w/o C.H.
- KOHL, Atman V.; B: 1891; D: 9-19-1936; Ψ World War.
- KOHL, Burna Fay; B: 12-21-1896; D: 5-10-1915; w/o Atman V.
- KOHL, E.V.; B: 1849.
- KOHL, Louisa M.; B: 1851; D: 1909.
- KOHL, Mary; B: 1853.
- KOHL, Netha; (no dates).
- KOHL, Solomon F., "Father"; B: 1845; D: 1935; Ψ Civil War.
- KOHL, William F.; B: 1880; D: 2-25-1928.
- KOOLBECK, John; B: 1841; D: 1923; Ψ Civil War.

- KOOLBECK, Rebecca Caroline; B: 1844; D: 1919.
- KRAUTZ, Ruban; (no dates).
- KROGH, --; (no dates); w/o Harold.
- KROGH, Loren M.; B: 1900; D: 1926.
- KROGH, Andrew Peter; D: 3-7-1938.
- KRUGLE, Mrs. --; (no dates).
- LAGE, Carl; B: 1860; D: 1926.
- LAGE, Cecilia; B: 1857; D: 1937.
- LAGE, Elise; B: 1871; D: 3-30-1895; w/o Johnnie.
- LAHR, Henry; B: 1854; D: 8-18-1930.
- LAKE, Effie; B: 1846; D: 10-2-1888; w/o Willis.
- LAMASTER, Walter Scott; B: 1877; D: 1934.
- LAMM, Henry; B: 1855; D: 1934.
- LANDON, Charles R.; B: 1876; D: 10-27-1906.
- LANDON, S.; (no dates).
- LARSEN, --; B: 1863; D: 1931; w/o Jeppe.
- LARSEN, Ellen M.; B: 1872; D: 6-19-1905; w/o Marinus.
- LARSEN, Hans; B: 1856; D: 1919.
- LARSEN, Jeppe; B: 1858; D: 1924.
- LARSEN, Mary; B: 1869; D: 1923.
- LARSEN, S.; (no dates).
- LATTA, J.W.; B: 1848; D: 5-14-1886.
- LAUGHMAN, Emily C.; B: 1849; D: 1922.
- LAUGHMAN, William; B: 1838; D: 1928; Ψ Civil War
- LAWSON, Henry; B: 1844; D: 1-6-1888; Ψ Civil War.
- LAWSON. Ester A.; B: 1844; D: 6-6-1888.
- LEDWICH, Bessie; D: 8-2-1882.
- LEDWICH, Elisa Shaw; B: 1839; D: 6-4-1909.
- LEDWICH, Elm; D: 11-27-1875; Age 111.
- LEDWICH, Evelyn G.; B: 1849; D: 1921.
- LEDWICH, John; B: 1814; D: 3-30-1898.
- LEDWICH, Le Grant; B: 1865; D: 7-13-1908.
- LEDWICH, May; D: 12-16-1877.
- LEDWICH, Sake; D: 5-20-1880.
- LEDWICH, Thomas; B: 1841; D: 7-8-1885; Ψ Civil War.
- LeRITTE, Birdella M.; B: 1889; D: 1921.
- LEUCH, Angeline; B: 1877; D: 1934; w/o Mike.

- LEUCH, Michael; B: 1871; D: 1935.
- LEUCH, Sophia W.; B: 1851; D: 1913; w/o H.H.
- LEUCH, Zerilon; B: 1847; D: 1937.
- LEWIS, Ely P.; B: 1876, Mahaska Co., Ia.; D: 2-7-1937; h/o Pearl Thompson.
- LEWIS, Ignatius S.; B: 1835; D: 3-22-1912; h/o Mary J.; Ψ Civil War.
- LEWIS, L.C.; (no dates).
- LEWIS, Mary J.; [no dates]; w/o Ignatius S.
- LEWIS, Mrs. C.C.; (no dates).
- LEWIS, William J.; B: 1892; D: 1937.
- LIGHTY, Floyd L.; B: 1873; D: 1910.
- LITTLETON, Ellen; B: 1859; D: 1902; w/o Geo.
- LITTLETON, George D.; B: 1836; D: 1913.
- LITTLETON, Jennie D., "Mother"; B: 1864; D: 1931.
- LLOYD, Anna B.; B: 1878; D: 11-7-1908; d/o R.E.
- LLOYD, Martha E.; B: 1847; D: 1926.
- LLOYD, Richard E.; B: 1849; D: 1918.
- LON[G]COR, Sarah J.; B: 1831; D: 5-1-1902; w/o P.H.
- LONG, James M.; B: 1818; D: 1889.
- LONG, John W.; B: 1872; D: 1923.
- LONG, Samantha; B: 1851; D: 2-1-1905.
- LONG, T.A.; (no dates); Ψ Civil War.
- LORENZ, Bruno; B: 1877; D: 1936.
- LORENZ, Ida; B: 1881; D: 1933.
- LOUDEN, Alvin L.; B: 1896; D: 1940; Ψ World War.
- LOUIS, J.H.; B: 1841; D: 1-9-1909; Ψ Civil War.
- LOUIS, Fannie B. Fetter; B: 1849; D: 9-17-1935.
- LOW, Jos.; B: 1808; D: 6-29-1878.
- LUCH, A.P.; B: 1847; D: 1927.
- LUECKE, Clarence H.; B: 1882; D: 1930.
- LUECKE, Herman H.; B: 1840; D: 1920.
- LUND, Chris N.; B: 1838; D: 1922.
- LUND, Elsie M.; B: 1846; D: 1920.
- LUXFORD, Mary A.; (no dates).
- LYNCH, Elizabeth; B: 1837; D: 3-26-1897; w/o Milton.
- LYNCH, Milton; B: 1829; D: 4-12-1898; Ψ Civil War.

- MA[CKRI]LL; Rose Cuppy; B: 1880; D: 1907.
- MAASSEN, John F.; B: 1868; D: 1-4-1931.
- MacMURRAY, Robinson; B: 1879; D: 2-1-1915.
- MacMURRAY, Robinson; B: 1879; D: 8-1-1915.
- MADISON, Martin [N.]; B: 1864; D: 1913.
- MADISON, Mary E.; B: 1866; D: 1916.
- MADSEN, Edna Nora; B: 1899; D: 1927.
- MADSEN, James; B: 1862; D: 5-21-1910.
- MADSEN, Lars; B: 1854; D: 1928.
- MADSEN, Nles [Nels]; B: 1860; D: 1926.
- MALCOM, Melissa A.; B: 1857; D: 4-17-1880; w/o Geo.
- MALICK, F.A. (Dr.); B: 1866; D: 7-17-1903.
- MALICK, Jeremiah M.; B: 1836; D: 1-28-1913; Ψ Civil War.
- MALICK, Mary E.; B: 1840; D: 8-30-1917.
- MARSON, Emma; B: 1855; D: 1922.
- MARTIN, Bertha N.; B: 1864; D: 11-3-1906.
- MARTIN, E.L.; B: 1861; D: 1932.
- MARTIN, E.M.; B: 1830; D: 1-12-1906.
- MARTIN, Elisa A.; B: 1837; D: 6-23-1920.
- MARTIN, Emma Jane; B: 1863; D: 1929; w/o E.L.
- MARTINSON, Fred; B: 1882; D: 1918.
- MAVIS, Frances A.; B: 1835; D: 3-1-1907; w/o John.
- MAVIS, John; B: 1826; D: 2-23-1897.
- MAVIS, William; (no dates).
- MAXWELL, Alexander; B: 1841; D: 3-30-1897.
- MAYNE, Alfred; B: 1875; D: 8-14-1899.
- MAYNE, Mary J.; B: 1849; D: 5-22-1904; w/o John S.
- MAYNE, John S., "Father"; B: 1843; D: 1-6-1928.
- McALL, Anna; B: 1855; D: 1920.
- McCALL, --; B: 1838; D: 1916.
- McCAULEY, --; B: 1839; D: 11-3-1924; w/o John.
- McCAULEY, Rev. John; B: 1840; D: 1899.
- McCONNELL, Jos. of Jas. [??]; B: 1842; D: 9-31-1886; Ψ Civil War.
- McCONNELL, Sarah; B: 1846; D: 2-6-1915; w/o J.
- McCONNELL, Webb; (no dates).
- McCORD, Alexander; B: 1811; D: 7-15-1887.
- McCORD, Arthur V.; B: 1-20-1881; D: 8-12-1912.

- McCORD, Bradley; B: 1852; D: 10-24-1919.
- McCORD, Mary E.; B: 1848; D: 1-19-1929.
- McCORY, Cornelius V.; B: 1858; D: 10-2-1919; Ψ Civil War.
- McCOY, Amelia; B: 1789; D: 8-23-1862.
- McCOY, E.B.; (no dates).
- McCOY, L.E.; (no dates).
- McDONALD, Thos. Corley; B: 1876; D: 1913; Ψ Spanish-American.
- McDOWELL, Albert L.; B: 1865; D: 1934.
- McDOWELL, Cora; (no dates).
- McDOWELL, H.M.; B: 1842; D: 1931.
- McDOWELL, Hattie B.; B: 1867; D: 7-16-1908.
- McDOWELL, Roy; (no dates).
- McDOWELL, Rufus K.; B: 1858; D: 5-8-1881.
- McDOWELL, Russell; (no dates).
- McDOWELL, Sarah S.; B: 1845; D: 1916.
- McGRAW, Aden A.; B: 1861; D: 4-24-1937.
- McGRAW, Lillian; B: 1868; D: 9-19-1937.
- McKEIG, Charles E.; B: 1869; D: 1939.
- McKEIG, Goldie; B: 1893; D: 1934; w/o Harold.
- McKEIG, J.W.; B: 1860; D: 1928.
- McKEIG, Margaret; B: 1865; D: 1934.
- McKEIG, Maud M.; B: 1783; D: 1925.
- McKEIGHAN, John; (no dates).
- McKEIGHAN, William; B: 1879, Kewane[e], Ill.; D: 4-3-1939; res. Harlan, Ia.; Co.B; Nonp. Pg 10, col 3, 4-6-1939 [??].
- McKINSEY, Fred; (no dates).
- McLIMANS, N.L.; (no dates); Ψ Co.C 20th Wis. Inf.
- McMILLAN, A.; B: 1809; D: 3-4-1881.
- McMILLAN, Amanda A.; B: 1822; D: 10-14-1888; w/o A.
- McMILLEN, J.M.; B: 1847; D: 2-24-1886.
- McMILLEN, Sarah; B: 1824; D: 4-4-1894; w/o T.
- McMILLEN, T.; B: 1819; D: 5-13-1894.
- McMILLEN, Wm. Preston; B: 1849; D: 8-10-1898.
- McMULLEN, David; B: 1819; D: 5-17-1897.
- McMULLEN, Elizabeth; B: 1825; D: 6-10-1900; w/o David.
- McMULLEN, Phoebe C.; B: 1859; D: 8-9-1922; w/o C.R.
- McMULLEN, Rosa A.; B: 1862; D: 11-3-1884; w/o C.E.

- McMULLEN, Sarah A.; B: 1847; D: 8-1-1919; d/o D. & E.
- McQUEEN, Geo. Jr.; D: 6-22-1931.
- McQUEEN, George; B: 1834; D: 3-2-1907; Ψ Co.C 22nd Ia. Inf.
- McQUEEN, Nancy J.; B: 1842; D: 3-24-1916; w/o Geo.
- MERRELL, Albert Riley; B: 1854; D: 9-21-1934.
- MERRELL, Ida Eliza; B: 1855; D: 12-11-1925.
- MERRILL, Jos. W.; B: 1867; D: 1919.
- MERRILL, Nancy Childres; B: 1828; D: 1912.
- MERRILL, Olive Ester; D: 1906.
- MERRILL, Ruth Ida; B: 5-9-1887; D: 11-11-1904.
- MERRITT, Mrs. --; (no dates).
- MERSHON, Hester; B: 1816; D: 2-2-1893; w/o J.W.
- MERSHON, J.W.; B: 1851; D: 1925.
- MICHAELSON, Christen; B: 1847; D: 11-10-1915.
- MICHAELSON, Mary; B: 1844; D: 6-8-1927; w/o Christen.
- MIKKELSEN, Andrew; B: 1851; D: 1923.
- MIKKELSEN, J.O.; B: 1854; D: 9-1-1922.
- MIKKELSEN, Karen; B: 1855; D: 1934.
- MIKKELSEN, Marthena; B: 1853; D: 2-19-1916.
- MILLER, --; (no dates); w/o Isaac.
- MILLER, Ada C.; B: 1860; D: 4-11-1914.
- MILLER, D.E.; B: 1860; D: 1923.
- MILLER, Emma J.; B: 1858; D: 1917; w/o Thos. J.
- MILLER, Ermalt; B: 1886; D: 1936; w/o R.W.
- MILLER, Flora J.; B: 1860; D: 4-24-1927.
- MILLER, George H.; B: 1858; D: 1928.
- MILLER, Glenn (Dr.); B: 1891; D: 1936.
- MILLER, Ira E.; B: 1889; D: 1930.
- MILLER, Isaac; B: 1847; D: 7-31-1906.
- MILLER, J.C.; B: 1852; D: 1935.
- MILLER, Judson Pence; B: 1851; D: 6-1-1906.
- MILLER, Lyddie; B: 1854; D: 1922; w/o G.C.
- MILLER, Maggie E.; B: 1861; D: 1921; w/o John C.
- MILLER, Mattie E.; B: 1863; D: 1938.
- MILLER, Thomas J.; B: 1849; D: 1910.
- MILLS, Vania; B: 1858; D: 1929.
- MOLLER, Loren J.; B: 1828; D: 3-19-1915.

- MOLLER, Mitte M.; B: 1837; D: 1-26-1911; w/o Loren J.
- MOORE, E.B. (Dr.) (Edwin); B: 1848; D: 1912; h/o Sarah E. Watters.
- MOORE, G.W.; (no dates).
- MOORE, Sarah E. (Watters); B: 1848; D: 1927; [w/o Edwin].
- MOOREHOUSE, Wilbur A.; B: 1865; D: 1930.
- MORGAN, Hannah Jane; B: 1849; D: 3-27-1927.
- MORGAN, I.M.; B: 1849; D: 1927; h/o Mary S.
- MORGAN, I.N.; B: 1844; D: 10-6-1915.
- MORGAN, John Welch; B: 1848; D: 3-2-1934.
- MORGAN, Louisa S.; B: 5-23-1885; D: 2-27-1923.
- MORGAN, Mary S.; B: 1853; D: 9-6-1908; w/o I.M.
- MORRIS; Margaret Kinney; B: 1822; D: 1907.
- MORTENSEN, Martin; B: 1895; D: 11-13-1939; Ψ World War.
- MORTENSEN, Mary; B: 1845; D: 1915.
- MORTENSEN, Peter; B: 1831; D: 1902.
- MUCK, Robert W.; B: 1832; D: 1917.
- MUCK, Susan Kohle; B: 1840; D: 1926.
- MUFIELD, Clem; B: 1873; D: 1913.
- MULDOON, Mary (Rudy)[Reidy]; (no dates).
- MURPHY, Grant; B: 1865; D: 11-25-1932.
- MUSSELMAN, --; B: 1841; D: 11-30-1911; w/o Daniel.
- MUSSELMAN, Arthur; B: 1883; D: 1907.
- MUSSELMAN, Daniel; B: 1834; D: 1899.
- MYATT, Frank; B: 1868; D: 1917.
- NANCE, Addo; (no dates).
- NANCE, Emma; (no dates).
- NANCE, F.M.; B: 1829; D: 1901.
- NANCE, I.S.; B: 1836; D: 1916.
- NEARY, Mary A.; B: 1860; D: 1923.
- NELSON, --; D: 1931; w/o Herman.
- NELSON, Anibe; B: 1877; D: 10-29-1908; w/o L.H.
- NELSON, Anna M.; B: 1842; D: 1926.
- NELSON, Anna Mary; B: 1871; D: 12-17-1907; w/o T.K.
- NELSON, C.; B: 1842; D: 1930.
- NELSON, C.U.; B: 1835; D: 1917.
- NELSON, Christine; B: 1827; D: 5-7-1916; w/o Fred'k.

- NELSON, Fred; D: 6-23-1939.
- NELSON, Frederick, "Father"; B: 1825; D: 2-15-1900.
- NELSON, Hora[c]e Manly; B: 1900; D: 1-2-1920; s/o W.H. & P.E.
- NELSON, Johanna L.; B: 1852; D: 1931.
- NELSON, Julius; B: 1858; D: 1928.
- NELSON, L.H.; B: 1868; D: 1-20-1938.
- NELSON, Loren P.; B: 1848; D: 1930.
- NELSON, M.; B: 1849; D: 1922; w/o P.T.
- NELSON, Marie, "Mother"; B: 1830; D: 1905.
- NELSON, Marie; B: 1879; D: 9-1-1911; w/o T.K.
- NELSON, Martha; B: 1[8]79; D: 8-27-1922; w/o N.B.
- NELSON, Mary H.; B: 1859; D: 1920.
- NELSON, Millwright; B: 1835; D: 1926.
- NELSON, N. Peter; B: 1878; D: 1933.
- NELSON, N.P.; B: 1870; D: 1921.
- NELSON, Nellie G.; B: 1874; D: 1929; w/o Chris.
- NELSON, Nells; B: 1858, Denmark; D: 10-22-1937.
- NELSON, P.T.; B: 1845; D: 1932.
- NELSON, Pearle E.; B: 1876; D: 5-27-1907; w/o W.H.
- NELSON, Rose; (no dates).
- NELSON, T.K.; B: 1864; D: 7-18-1928.
- NEUMEYER, Carrie W.; B: 1859; D: 11-3-1898; w/o H.K.
- NEWBY, Eliza Fairfield; B: 1852; D: 1919.
- NEWBY, J.T.; B: 1873; D: 1938.
- NEWBY, James A.; B: 1856; D: 6-9-1874.
- NEWBY, James; B: 1825; D: 9-15-1905.
- NEWBY, Joseph W.; B: 1849; D: 1915.
- NEWBY, Julia; B: 1822; D: 5-26-1904.
- NEWBY, Lydia J.; B: 1846; D: 1899.
- NIELSEN, George G.; B: 3-22-1908; D: 6-2-1926.
- NIELSEN, Jens A.; B: 1863; D: 1932.
- NIELSEN, Kirstine M.; B: 1872; D: 8-3-1918.
- NIELSEN, Nettie; B: 1862; D: 1922; w/o Thos.
- NIELSEN, Niels; B: 1862; D: 1930.
- NIELSEN, Thomas; B: 1856; D: 1924.
- NOBLE, Althea E.; B: 1861; D: 1-17-1936.
- NOBLE, E.P.; B: 4-14-1856; D: 12-14-1922.

- NOBLE, Esther; B: 1844; D: 1912; w/o J.
- NOBLE, Peter Jr.; (no dates).
- NOBLE, Peter; B: 1831; D: 1913.
- NOBLE, Susan; B: 1836; D: 5-3-1889; w/o Peter.
- NOBLE, Vera Thimm; B: 1902; D: 1926; w/o Bert.
- NOLLEN, Michael; B: 1865; D: 1939.
- NOLLEN. Effie; B: 1867; D: 1936.
- NORGAARD, Jens; B: 1862; D: 10-25-1923.
- NORTON, Joseph; B: 1825, NY State; D: 3-14-1908; Burial record; Avoca Journal Herald, 3-19-1908.
- NUTTER, Wm. H.; B: 1815; D: 1-30-1879.
- NYMAN, Virginia Rose (O'Bucht); B: 1900; D: 1928.
- NYRUP, Catherine; B: 1869; D: 1929.
- O'BANION, Evaline; B: 1835; D: 8-3-1893; w/o J.W.
- O'BRECHT, Alta Elizabeth; B: 1898; D: 1928.
- O'BRECHT, C.A.; B: 1868; D: 8-10-1917; h/o Jennie Plummer.
- O'NIEL, Chas D.; B: 1847; D: 6-19-1922; Ψ Co.A 134th Ia. Inf.
- O'NIEL, S.A.; B: 1852; D: 1914; w/o Chas. D.
- OAKS, Elisha D.; B: 1845; D: 1926.
- OAKS, Jennie P.; B: 1842; D: 1933.
- OAKS, Salmon; B: 1802; D: 1883.
- OER, Fred A.; B: 3-17-1898; D: 2-9-1924; Ψ World War.
- OLSEN, Christen; B: 1853; D: Dec 1900.
- OLSEN, Edward; B: 1882; D: 1939.
- OLSEN, Hulda A.; B: 1879; D: 1925; w/o Lars.
- OSBORN, Clara; B: 1849; D: 8-2-1902.
- OSBORN, Cora L.; D: 1-27-1928.
- OSBORN, Jennie J.; D: 6-4-1935.
- OVERFIELD, M.S.; B: 1860; D: 1928.
- OVERHOLT, Carrie Noble; D: 1-22-1940.
- OVERHOLT, Eleanor E.; D: 6-21-1869.
- OVERHOLT, Eleanor; B: 1844; D: 1914; w/o Ira B.
- OVERHOLT, Frank (Dr.); B: 1835; D: 6-22-1865.
- OVERHOLT, Ira B.; B: 1833; D: 1928.
- OVERSON, Ole; B: 3-1-1897; D: 12-13-1939; Ψ World War.
- PARDEE, Edw. L.; B: 1836; D: 4-10-1911; Ψ Co.G 22nd Ia. Inf.
- PARDEE, Marinda E.; B: 1842; D: 12-13-1923; w/o Edw. L.

- PARKER, Ekor George [George Eokars]; B: 1903; D: 1933.
- PARKER, Elizabeth (Eokars); B: 1871; D: 1917; w/o A.V. Parker.
- PARKER, John G.; D: 7-8-1936.
- PARKER, Ruth Condon; B: 1847; D: 1940.
- PARKER, Walter Rush; B: 1843; D: 1922; Ψ Civil War.
- PASCOE, Ella; B: 1855; D: 8-17-1925.
- PATTEE, Elmira J. Lytton, "Mother"; B: 1865; D: 1927.
- PATTEE, Minerva J.; B: 1853; D: 3-9-1900.
- PATTERSON, Estella B.; B: 1875; D: 8-20-1907.
- PATTERSON, Ida Mae; B: 1872; D: 1926.
- PATTERSON, Luella D.; B: 1873; D: 1902.
- PAUL, Dallas F.; B: 1845; D: 12-6-1889; Ψ Co.G 115th [NY Inf.].
- PAUL, Edith; B: 1848; D: 9-4-1917.
- PAULSEN, Aug. C.; B: 1857; D: 12-2-1895.
- PAUP, Clifford; B: 1881; D: 1914.
- PAUP, George; B: 1833; D: 3-16-1905.
- PAUP, Goldie E.; B: 1884; D: 1917.
- PAUP, Harry L.; B: 1894; D: 1932; Ψ World War.
- PAUP, Horatio H.; B: 1857; D: 2-17-1923.
- PAUP, Joe H.; B: 1861; D: 1933.
- PAUP, Julia A.; B: 1825; D: 1912.
- PAUP, W.P.; (no dates).
- PAUP, Wm. L[e]slie; B: 1853; D: 11-27-1920.
- PEIFFER, Gaverni; B: 1880; D: 6-16-1918.
- PERFECT, D.V.; B: 1851; D: 5-12-1923; w/o L.B.
- PERFECT, L.A.; (no dates).
- PERFECT, S.B.; B: 1845; D: 5-11-1935.
- PERRY, James P.; B: 1842; D: 5-3-1893; Ψ Civil War.
- PERRY, Mary; B: 1847; D: 3-18-1901.
- PERRY, Wm. Grant; B: 1869; D: 3-17-1890.
- PETERS, Tracy; D: 1939.
- PETERSEN, Hannah; B: 1880; D: 1905.
- PETERSEN, Mannus C.; B: 1878; D: 1930.
- PETERSEN, Mary; B: 1882; B: 1934; w/o Jens M.
- PETERSEN, N.P.; B: 1856; D: 1926.
- PETERSEN, Nite K.; B: 1848; D: 1919.
- PETERSEN, Peder H. [G.?]; (no dates).

- PETERSEN, Peter I., "Father"; B: 1846; D: 1911.
- PETERSEN, Peter S., "Father"; B: 1863; D: 1933.
- PETERSEN, Tony; D: 3-11-1940.
- PETERSON, "Father"; B: 1866; D: 1920.
- PETERSON, Anna; B: 1861; D: 1891.
- PETERSON, Knud; B: 1858; D: 2-11-1887.
- PETERSON, Simon; B: 1834; D: 4-15-1921.
- PEXTON, J.F.; B: 1863; D: 1938.
- PFISTER, Frank; B: 1864; D: 1932.
- PFISTER, Mamie B.; B: 1895; D: 1918.
- PHILLIPS, David; B: 1836; D: 2-7-1914.
- PHILLIPS, Emeline C.; B: 1840; D: 6-20-1908.
- PHILLIPS, Francis E.; B: 1866; D: 1937.
- PHILSON, S.J.; B: 1874; D: 1915.
- PICKARD, Fred W., "Father"; B: 1862; D: 1937.
- PICKARD, Leigh H.; B: 1884; D: 1896; Age 12.
- PICKARD, Lulu M.; B: 1872; D: 1901.
- PICKARD, Luther H.; B: 1844; D: 1-18-1922; Ψ Civil War.
- PICKARD, Mary F.; B: 1845; D: 1919.
- PICKARD, Pearl Edith; B: 1891; D: 1929.
- PICKARD, S.O.; B: 1816; D: 1896.
- PICKERING, Sarah E.; B: 1867; D: 1919.
- PIERCE, George D.; B: 1848; D: 1930.
- PIERCE, Grace; B: 1891; D: 1914.
- PIPER, Martha; B: 1853; D: 1892.
- PLATT, Elizabeth; (no dates); w/o J.F.
- PLATT, James T.; B: 1842; D: 7-20-1927.
- PLUMB, --; (no dates); w/o Robert F.
- PLUMB, Alfred A.; B: 1881; D: 1930.
- PLUMB, Charlotte; B: 1837; D: 1920.
- PLUMB, Frank; B: 1846; D: 1931.
- PLUMB, Grace; B: 1845; D: 1928.
- PLUMB, John E.; B: 1870; D: 6-10-1905.
- PLUMB, Robert F.; B: 1872; D: 1930.
- PLUMB, Valentine; B: 1843; D: 1935.
- PLUMMER, Samuel C.; B: 1845; D: 4-22-1917.
- PLUMMER, Sarah C.; B: 1856; D: 1-9-1916; w/o S.C.

- POLING, Ella; (no dates).
- POLING, M.; B: 1819; D: 1-13-1907; Ψ Co.B 13th Ia. Inf.
- POLING, Martha Ella; B: 1857; D: 1-25-1893; w/o G.C.
- POOLE, Francis; B: 1810; D: 7-16-1882.
- POOLE, Mary C.; B: 1841; D: 12-9-1917.
- POOLE, Samuel G.; B: 1841; D: 9-24-1914; Ψ Co.C 11th O. Inf.
- PORTER, Melinda Fisher; B: 1834; D: 4-27-1907.
- POSHWATTS, Anna Maria; B: 1891; D: 10-10-1912.
- POTTER, Caleb F.; B: 1838; D: 12-9-1913.
- POTTER, Cynthia A.; B: 1844; D: 4-7-1915.
- POTTER, E.S.; B: 1857; D: 1-10-1884.
- POTTER, Frank E.; B: 1865; D: 1932.
- POTTER, Grace Janette; B: 7-8-1893; D: 1-11-1914.
- POTTER, J.N.; B: 1806; D: 12-14-1886.
- POTTER, L.F.; B: 1855, Wis.; D: 4-8-1928.
- POTTER, Martha; B: 1857; D: 1914; w/o L.F.
- POTTER, Mattie S.; B: 1874; D: 1927.
- PRATT, Sisney K.; B: 1859; D: 4-28-1893.
- PRITCHARD, Alexander; B: 1847; D: 5-14-1907.
- PRITCHARD, Edw. Albert; B: 1880; D: 1938.
- PRITCHARD, Hugh R.; B: 11-6-1882; D: 7-30-1931.
- PRITCHARD, Mary; B: 1847; D: 6-26-1921.
- PULVER, Clementine; B: 1865; D: 1926; w/o Chas.
- RACELY, William H.; D: 5-16-1883; Ψ Co.I 7th Wis.
- RADCLIFFE, John A.; B: 1785; D: 3-1-1910. [?]
- RAINBOW, E.C.; B: 1856; D: 4-14-1885.
- RAINS, Henry C.; B: 1859; D: 2-3-1895.
- RAMSAY, Eliza M.; B: 1837; D: 1-3-1909.
- RAMSAY, James Oliver; B: 1839; D: 12-8-1904.
- RAMSEY, Catherine; B: 1822; D: 2-5-1922.
- RAMSEY, Fred J.; B: 1891; D: 1923; Ψ World War.
- RAMSEY, John; B: 1827; D: 5-21-1901.
- RASSMUSSEN, Chris; B: 1861; D: 1936.
- RASSMUSSEN, Marie; B: 1848; D: 3-4-1908; w/o C.C.
- RECORDS, Mallie L.; B: 1848; D: 9-8-1908; m/o D.H.
- REHDER, Anna; B: 1865; D: 6-23-1916; 1st [2nd] w/o August.
- REHDER, Anna; B: 1878; D: 5-23-1904; 2nd [1st] w/o August.

- REHDER, August; B: 1861; D: 1934.
- REINHART, Alban S.; B: 1854; D: 1918.
- REINHART, Charles H.; B: 3-8-1888; D: 9-7-1926; Ψ World War.
- REYELT, A.D., "Father"; B: 1862; D: 1927.
- REYELT, Alfred V.; B: 1893; D: 1918.
- REYELT, Helmer E.; B: 1895; D: 1918; Ψ World War.
- REYELT, Jessie W.; B: 1897; D: 1918; w/o Alfred.
- REYNOLDS, J.H.; B: 1843; D: 4-7-1927; Ψ Civil War.
- REYNOLDS, Lucy M.; B: 1845; D: 8-25-1909.
- REYNOLDS, Ressa M.; B: 1871; D: 12-26-1904.
- REYNOLDS, Robert L.; B: 1883; D: 12-18-1912.
- ROBERTS, Eliza A.; B: 1843; D: 1881; w/o B.
- ROBERTS, Hannah; B: 1848; D: 2-26-1888; w/o Wm.
- ROBERTS, Sarah Tague; B: 1843; D: 1915; w/o William.
- ROBERTS, William; B: 1844; D: 1925.
- ROBINSON, J. Fred; B: 1869; D: 10-12-1908.
- ROBINSON, Julia A.; B: 1839; D: 9-16-1910; w/o T.J.
- ROBINSON, T.J.; B: 1832; D: 10-14-1893; Ψ Co.C 36th Ia. Inf.
- ROCKWELL, Neomia C.; B: 1849; D: 3-4-1887.
- RODGERS, Beulah C.; B: 1884; D: 1907; w/o C.
- RODGERS; T.G.; (no dates); Also his wife --   .
- ROLAND, Abner John; B: 1874; D: 11-9-1903.
- ROLD, --; (no dates); w/o Nels.
- ROLD, --; (no dates); Ψ World War.
- ROLD, Charlotte M.; B: 184[0]; D: 9-29-1900.
- ROLD, Christine; (no dates).
- ROLD, Jens P.C.; B: 1839; D: 5-14-1929.
- ROLD, John J.; B: 1871; D: 1927.
- ROLD, Mary; B: 1867; D: 1923.
- ROSENKILDE, Agnes; B: 1898; D: 1928.
- ROSS, Emily O.; B: 1844; D: 11-28-1904; w/o G[eo] D.
- ROSS, George Dallas; B: 1842; D: 3-24-1925; Ψ Civil War.
- ROSS, Rose E.; B: 1878; D: 5-25-1925; w/o W.L. Fisher.
- ROUZER, Anna L.; B: 1863; D: 5-22-1918.
- RUFFCORN, Frank Leander; B: 1874; D: 10-17-1928.
- RUFFCORN, Howard Dale; B: 6-25-1910; D: 2-23-1930.
- RUFFCORN, P.H.; B: 1844; D: 9-5-1932; Ψ Co.B 85th Pa. Inf.

- RUFFCORN, Wayne Oliver; B: 1894; D: 8-15-1923; s/o P.H.
- SAHL, Carrie M.; B: 1860; D: 1928.
- SAHL, Christian I.; B: 1856; D: 1929.
- SALTER, Janette (Maxwell); B: 1870; D: 1903.
- SARGENT, Catherine; B: 1852; D: 3-11-1889; w/o B.
- SARGENT, Letitia; B: 1836; D: 1928.
- SARGENT, Peheb; B: 1866; D: 1917; w/o W.H.
- SARGENT, Philli[p]; B: 1899; D: 1918.
- SARGENT, William; D: 4-11-1939; Age 82; Ψ Co.B.
- SAWYERS, Sarah T.; B: 1855; D: 8-14-1906; w/o J.C.
- SCHOUBOE, Claudius S.; B: 1855; D: 10-15-1898.
- SCHOUBOE, Petrine; B: 1850; D: 4-29-1890.
- SCHOUBOE, Sophie Anderson; B: 1861; D: 1927; w/o C.
- SCHUMAKER, John D.; B: 1841; D: 1920.
- SCHWAB, --; (no dates).
- SCHWAB, Johanna C.; B: 1856; D: 1918.
- SCUTT, Wesley; B: 1843; D: 1923.
- SEEGER, Max Wilhelm; B: 1878; D: 1936.
- SEEGER, Minnie Belle; B: 1871; D: 1936.
- SEELAND, Johanna D.; B: 1855; D: 4-7-1936.
- SEITEL, Louis J.; B: 1857; D: 1931.
- SEITEL, Phillip; B: 1855; D: 9-28-1928.
- SELLERS, Frank Edgar; B: 1866; D: 1915.
- SELLERS, Nina J.; B: 1872; D: 12-9-1902.
- SETTER, J.W.; B: 1845; D: 1902.
- SETTER, Nettie A. Fisher; B: 1856; D: 1926.
- SHAFER, Mary A.; B: 1840; D: 1915; w/o P.
- SHAFER, Phillip; B: 1841; D: 9-26-1896.
- SHAFER, Rosa E.; (no dates).
- SHAW, Benjamin; B: 1868; D: 1938.
- SHEPHERD, --; B: 1835; D: 1908; w/o J.F.
- SHEPHERD, Cor[a] S. (Ramsey); B: 1864; D: 1922; w/o W.T.
- SHEPHERD, James Farquhar, B: 1821; D: 1903.
- SHEPHERD, Wm. Thos.; B: 1863; D: 1931.
- SHOEMAKER, Arminda; B: 1848; D: 1919; w/o Geo. A.
- SHOEMAKER, George H.; B: 1844; D: 1921; Ψ GAR marker.
- SHULTZ, Abel L.; B: 1867; D: 1927.

- SIMMS, Vern M.; B: 5-10-1896; D: 8-7-1929; Ψ World War.
- SIMONSEN, Betty Jane; D: 7-14-1938.
- SMITH, Annie (Sheppard); B: 1837; D: 3-22-1881; w/o R.M.
- SMITH, Arabella E.; B: 1842; D: 6-26-1887; w/o N.S.
- SMITH, Eugene J.; B: 1849; D: 1919.
- SMITH, Fred Arthur; B: 1874; D: 1921.
- SMITH, Hannah; B: 1868; D: 1933.
- SMITH, Harry G.; B: 1879; D: 1910.
- SMITH, Jennie C. (Stendrup); B: 1860; D: 2-2-1897; w/o Loren M.
- SMITH, Mary G.; B: 1850; D: 1915.
- SMITH, Mary J.; B: 1849; D: 1924; w/o L.C.
- SMITH, Nathaniel; B: 1837; D: 1-9-1874; Ψ Civil War.
- SMITH, R.M. (Dr.); B: 1834; D: 1879; Ψ Civil War.
- #SMITH, Rosa B. (White); B: 1868; D: 1936; w/o J.A. (Berry) Smith.
- SMITH, Thomas; B: 1854; D: 9-18-1936.
- SNYDER, Hulda E.; B: 1853; D: 1931; w/o W.M.
- SNYDER, William; B: 1849; D: 1924.
- SOESBE, Daniel; B: 1836; D: 9-4-1902.
- SOESBE, Harriett; B: 1836; D: 1922; w/o Daniel.
- SOESBE, Josephine; (no dates).
- SONDERGARD, Genevieve; B: 1905; D: 1937.
- SORENSEN, Else; B: 1838; D: 1923.
- SORENSEN, Esther M.; B: 1836; D: 1932.
- SORENSEN, James G.; B: 1852; D: 1933.
- SORENSEN, Jens; B: 1869; D: 1933.
- SORENSEN, June V. (Blair); B: 1900; D: 1928; w/o Gordon.
- SORENSEN, Karen; B: 1848; D: 1919; w/o M.
- SORENSEN, Katie; B: 1862; D: 9-18-1905; w/o A.S.
- SORENSEN, Lars P.; B: 1863; D: 8-13-1934.
- SORENSEN, Lars; B: 1873; D: 1927.
- SORENSEN, Loren [Soren?]; B: 1875; D: 1891.
- SORENSEN, Maggie, "Mother"; B: 1865; D: 1937.
- SORENSEN, Mary, "Mother"; B: 1869; D: 1930.
- SORENSEN, Mary; B: 1848; D: 5-5-1904; w/o Neils.
- SORENSEN, Michael C.; B: 1850; D: 1917.
- SORENSEN, Neils; B: 1851; D: 1918.

- SORENSEN, Nels Block; B: 1890; D: 1927.
- SORENSEN, Oliver; B: 4-13-1888; D: 11-25-1936; Ψ World War.
- SORENSEN, Peter L.; B: 1871; D: 1-2-1936.
- SORENSEN, Peter, "Father"; B: 1856; D: 1926.
- SORENSEN; Stine; B: 1866; D: 1937.
- SORENSON, A.S.; B: 1854; D: 1930.
- SORENSON, Alfred G.; B: 1879; D: 11-21-1918.
- SORENSON, Annie; D: 9-20-1904.
- SORENSON, Becca Rodl; B: 1874; D: 2-8-1927; w/o Nick.
- SORENSON, Carrie; D: 12-19-1882.
- SORENSON, Chris; B: 1842; D: 1910.
- SPARR, Mary; B: 1862; D: 4-5-1861.
- SPEICE, Nancy; B: 1830; D: 5-9-1904; w/o Nicholas.
- SPEICE, Nicholas; B: 1828; D: 6-29-1901.
- SPENCE, Guy Herman; B: 9-2-1896; D: 6-17-1919; Ψ World War.
- SPURGEON, Emily Wyland; B: 1877; D: 1935.
- SPURGEON, Sarah C.; B: 1849; D: 12-17-1911.
- SPURGEON, William H.; B: 1849; D: 10-18-1924.
- STAMM, Ellis L.; B: 1835; D: 5-10-1883; h/o Marie L.
- STAMM, Marie L.; B: 1835; D: 1913; w/o E.L.
- STANLEY, "Mother"; (no dates).
- STANLEY, Charles; B: 1876; D: 1935; Ψ Spanish-American War.
- STANLEY, J.L.; B: 1838; D: 5-26-1890.
- STANLEY, Samuel; (no dates).
- STANLEY, Thos. F.; B: 1865; D: 8-21-1881; s/o J.L. & L.J.
- STARLING, Alvaretta; B: 1860; D: 1928.
- STARLING, Oscar A.; B: 1859; D: 1925.
- STEELE, James C.; B: 1855; D: 1937.
- STEPHENSEN, Mary; B: 1887; D: 2-16-1904.
- STEWART, George E.; B: 1864; D: 1932.
- STEWART, Laura R.; (no dates); w/o Thos.
- STEWART, William; B: 1868; D: 1934.
- STILES, Amelia D.; B: 1847; D: 2-32-1879.
- STOLZ, Alois; B: 1855; D: 1934.
- STOLZ, Barbara; B: 1860; D: 1935.
- STOP, --; (no dates); w/o Everett.
- STUART, Sallie Annie Robbert; B: 1847; D: 1911.

- STUTZMAN, --; B: 1819; D: Dec 1908.
- STUTZMAN, Amasa M.; B: 1859; D: 4-18-1922.
- STUTZMAN, Jacob B.; B: 1834; D: 11-20-1922.
- STUTZMAN, Jonathan B.; B: 1819; D: 1908.
- STUTZMAN, Juliann; B: 1840; D: 8-8-1897.
- STUTZMAN, Mary Allen, B: 1855; D: 6-22-1930.
- STUTZMAN, Robert T.; B: 1849; D: 18[8]2.
- STUTZMAN, Sarah T.; B: 1830; D: 1901.
- STUTZMAN, William S.; B: 1852; D: 1896.
- SUMMERS, Myrtle, "Mother"; B: 1890; D: 1923.
- SUNDERLAND, L.D.; B: 1825, Fayette Co., O.; D: 4-17-1904.
- SUNDERLAND, Mary E.; B: 1834; D: 1-3-1909.
- SWARTZ, Samuel W.; B: 1835; D: 1902; Ψ Co.B 71st Ill. Inf.
- SWARTZ, Sarah Palgrove; B: 1834; D: 1916; w/o Sam'l.
- SWIFT, Carran Freeman; B: 1861; D: 1921.
- SWIFT, Louis; B: 1884; D: 6-16-1909.
- SWIFT, Tina E. Koolock; B: 1865; D: 1925; w/o C.F.
- SWIFT, William; B: 1852; D: 8-10-1896.
- SWINEHART, Elizabeth; B: 1854; D: 1937.
- SWINEHART, George; B: 1830; D: 1912.
- SWITZER, Ella; B: 1862; D: 1917; w/o Wm. Jr.
- SWITZER, Katherine; B: 1821; D: 3-5-1901; m/o Wm. Jr.
- SWITZER, William Sr.; B: 1818; D: 3-23-1901.
- SWITZER, William, (Jr.); B: 1856; D: 1922.
- TAGUE, Arthur Thos.; B: 1903; D: 1922.
- TAGUE, Arthur; D: 3-21-1937.
- TAGUE, Ephriam C. [Ephraim]; B: 1840; D: 5-27-1912.
- TAGUE, George; B: 1875; D: 1935.
- TAGUE, Jacob; B: 1849; D: 6-8-1926.
- TAGUE, James; D: 3-12-1929.
- TAGUE, Margaret J., "Mother"; B: 1879; D: 1932.
- TAGUE, Peree; B: 1851; D: 6-20-1914.
- TAGUE, Phebe Jane; B: 1848; D: 5-5-1917.
- TALLMAN, Gertrude; B: 1877; D: 3-27-1895.
- TALLMAN, James H.; B: 1846; D: 2-16-1905; Ψ Co.E 31st Ia. Inf.
- TALLMAN, Jennie L.; B: 1849; D: 12-11-1932; w/o James.
- TAYLOR, Charles M.; B: 1846; D: 7-10-1915; Ψ GAR marker.

- TAYLOR, Lieutellas S.; B: 1841; D: 9-4-1932.
- TAYLOR, Mary E.; B: 1848; D: 7-14-1920.
- TELTON, --; (no dates); w/o Geo.
- TELTON, Geo.; D: 12-26-1938.
- TERRILL, Daniel; B: 1861; D: 1939.
- THIAEN [THRAEN], Mary; B: 1882; D: 10-10-1929.
- THIMM, Aksel B.; B: 1905; D: 1926.
- THIMM, Jensima M., "Mother"; B: 1883; D: 1919.
- THIMM, John, "Father"; B: 1880; D: 1927.
- THOGERSEN, J. Chris; B: 1879; D: 1918.
- THOGERSEN, Lina; B: 1886; D: 1919; w/o Paul.
- THOISEN, Chris; B: 1866; D: 1925.
- THOMPSEN, "Mother"; B: 1835; D: 1916.
- THOMPSON, Eileen; B: 1917; D: 1939.
- THOMPSON, Lottie Gardner; B: 1888; D: 1927.
- THORNBURG, "Father"; B: 1864; D: 1934.
- THORNBURG, "Mother"; B: 1874; D: 1928.
- THORNBURG, Virgil, "Father"; B: 1894; D: 1928.
- TINSLEY, Alfred Dwight; B: 1854; D: 1923.
- TINSLEY, Frank; B: 1886; D: 1910.
- TINSLEY, Henry Ross; B: 1865; D: 11-18-1895.
- TINSLEY, Maria; B: 1857; D: 1937.
- TINSLEY, Prior; B: 1852; D: 1923.
- TOWNSON, Earl L.; B: 3-12-1896; D: 5-3-1922.
- TOWNSON, Urbanna E.; B: 1856; D: 1917; w/o W.H.
- TOWNSON, William H.; B: 1858; D: 1938.
- TRUMAN, Clark; B: 1808; D: 1892.
- TRUMAN, Eustice; B: 1843; D: 3-10-1877; w/o P.C.
- TUCK, Elizabeth; B: 1826; D: 12-20-1908.
- TUCK, John J.; B: 1821; D: 3-11-1890.
- TURNER, A[lexander] Elmer; B: 1861; D: 1923.
- TURNER, Caroline; B: 1840; D: 1916.
- TURNER, Jerome; D: 1-23-1904.
- TURPIN, Bertie; B: 1876; D: 9-30-1898; s/o G. & E.
- TURPIN, Emma; B: 1848; D: 5-30-1878; w/o Geo.
- TURPIN, George; B: 1846; D: 1920; Ψ Civil War.
- TURPIN, Julia; (no dates).

- TURPIN, Sarah; B: 1815; D: 11-6-1896; w/o Wm.
- TURPIN, William; B: 1807; D: 2-17-1896.
- VIGG, J.S.; B: 1862; D: 1926.
- VINCENT, Lee J.; D: 5-26-1922; Ψ World War.
- VINTON, Adolphus G. (see Gustavus Adolphus Vinton); B: 1826; D: 9-8-1914.
- VINTON, Alonzo R.; B: 1819; D: 5-1-1880.
- VINTON, Gustavus Adolphus; B: 1826, Cornish, N,H.; D: 9-8-1914; s/o Daniel & Huldah Smith.
- VOGT, Nicholas; B: 1823; D: 7-21-1892.
- VON TERSCH, Catherine; B: 1865; D: 5-14-1935.
- VON TERSCH, Joseph; B: 1847; D: 3-24-1930.
- WADE, Jacob B.; B: 1847; D: 12-26-1914; Ψ Civil War.
- WAGGONER, Delpha D.; B: 1907; D: 1934; w/o Chas.
- WAITE, Elon G.; B: 1811; D: 1-27-1887.
- WALLER, Geo. L.; B: 1836; D: 3-5-1902; Ψ Co.K 8th Pa. Cav.
- WALLER, Harry; (no dates); s/o Geo.
- WALLER, Louisa M.; B: 1847; D: 6-20-1935; w/o Geo.
- WALTERS, Abraham; B: 1852; D: 6-4-1916.
- WALTERS, Anna Long; B: 1874; D: 1938.
- WALTERS, Anthony; B: 1854; D: 1923.
- WALTERS, Arrena; B: 1826; D: 5-8-1891; w/o S.A.
- WALTERS, Cort C.; B: 1872; D: 1923.
- WALTERS, Daniel B.; B: 1823; D: 10-27-1903.
- WALTERS, Gottlieb; B: 1862; D: 1927.
- WALTERS, Jennie; B: 1858; D: 1927.
- WALTERS, Margaret E.; B: 1829; D: 11-3-1893; w/o Daniel B.
- WARD, Olice G.; B: 1845; D: 8-17-1905; w/o R.S.
- WARREN, Georgia M.; B: 1870; D: 12-8-1886; w/o T.J.
- WATERBURY, Francis; B: 1846, Illinois; D: 1913; h/o Mary Wright.
- WATERBURY, Mary; B: 1848; D: 1914.
- WATERS, Carrie Harvey; B: 1859; D: 9-4-1884.
- WATKINS, J.M.; B: 1849; D: 2-10-1921.
- WATKINS, Maggie J.; B: 1879; D: 11-3-1907.
- WATKINS, Sallie; B: 1841; D: 1916; w/o J.M.
- WEBER, Addie B.; B: 1870; D: 1937.
- WEBER, Charles C.; B: 1861; D: 1932.

- WEBER, Mary D.; B: 1836; D: 9-4-1884; w/o John Colner.
- WEEKS, Annabel Snowden; B: 1845; D: 1907.
- WEEKS, Harry Philbrick; B: 1872; D: 1-29-1911.
- WEEKS, J.H.; B: 1838; D: 12-29-1895; Ψ Co.I 32nd O. Inf.
- WEIGART, Elizabeth E.; B: 1856; D: 5-4-1912; w/o J.J.
- WEIGART, Lena, "Mother"; B: 1866; D: 1936
- WEIRICH, Geo.; B: 1852; D: 1901.
- WEIRICH, Max; B: 1887; D: 1908.
- WELSH, Nevada M.; B: 1869; D: 3-3-1900.
- WELSH, Paul H.; B: 1890; D: 1934; Ψ World War.
- WENTZ, Roberta Daley; B: 1888; D: 1921.
- WHITE, Bessie L.; B: 1885; D: 4-23-1930.
- WHITE, Charles O.; B: 1870; D: 1936.
- WHITE, Ellen N.; B: 1850; D: 7-6-1915; w/o O.L.
- WHITE, George E.; B: 1883; D: 1937.
- WHITE, J. Carl; B: 1888; D: 1932.
- WHITE, M.J.; B: 1876; D: 1920.
- WHITE, Nicholas Orville; B: 1889; D: 1918.
- WHITE, Nicholas; B: 1840; D: 1917; Ψ Co.L 4th Ia. Cav.
- WHITE, Quintin L.; B: 1853; D: 3-28-1917.
- WHITE, Rachel A.; B: 1846; D: 1922.
- WHITE, Ralph; (no dates).
- WHITNEY, Jack E.; B: 6-23-1918; D: 10-21-1935.
- WHITNEY, Jesse B.; B: 1863; D: 1927.
- WICK, Alvin H.; B: 1838; D: 2-12-1919; Ψ Co.H 5th U.S.Art.
- WICK, Emma E. (Ufford); B: 1848; D: 4-1-1928; w/o A.H.
- WICKERSHAM, Jobe O.; B: 1840; D: 1-1-1917; Ψ Co.A 122nd Ill. Vol.
- WICKERSHAM, Mary M.; B: 1847; D: 2-21-1931; w/o Jobe.
- WICKS, Albert; B: 1827; D: 4-25-1890.
- WICKS, Mary Stryker; B: 1836; D: 10-18-1907; w/o Albert.
- WICKS, Worth D.; B: 1853; D: 7-23-1892.
- WILCOX, --; D: 4-1-1939; w/o Roy.
- WILCOX, Andrew C.; B: 1833; D: 12-29-1910.
- WILCOX, Aurelia; B: 1870; D: 1884.
- WILCOX, Chester; B: 1872; D: 1926.
- WILCOX, Clade C.; B: 1842; D: 1934; w/o Andrew C.

- WILCOX, Fred Levi; B: 1883; D: 1918; Ψ World War.
- WILDER, Chas L.; B: 1840; D: 4-27-1895; Ψ Co.I 9th Ia. Inf.
- WILEY, Gertrude M., "Mother"; B: 1875; D: 1922.
- WILLIAMS, Mrs. --; (no dates).
- WILSON, Daniel A.; B: 1854; D: 7-1-1931.
- WILSON, Daniel, "Father"; B: 1818; D: 8-24-1890.
- WILSON, George F.; B: 1861; D: 4-15-1922.
- WILSON, Ida H.; B: 1859; D: 1-13-1904; w/o of Daniel A.
- WILSON, Jane Ann; B: 4-16-1913; D: 10-2-1909; w/o Daniel.
- WILSON, John; B: 1828; D: 11-26-1915.
- WILSON, Mary; B: 1812; D: 11-3-1889; w/o of W.L.
- WINDER, H.W.; B: 1838; D: 1931; Ψ Co.D 33rd Ia. Inf.
- WINDER, Mary E.; B: 1842; D: 1918; w/o E.W.
- WINEGAR, James Ellsworth; B: 1819; D: 7-1-1909.
- WIRTH, Charles F.; B: 1887; D: 1908.
- WIRTH, Ellen J.; B: 1865; D: 1939.
- WIRTH, Phillip L.; B: 1856; D: 1920.
- WOHLHUTTER, --; B: 1907; D: 1939.
- WOLFF, Alice J.; B: 1856; D: 7-18-1937; w/o Jno. W.
- WOLFF, John W.; B: 1849; D: 7-16-1905.
- WRAY, Dora; B: 1901; D: 1935; w/o Elmer.
- WRAY, Elmer Floyd; B: 1892; D: 1935; Ψ World War.
- WYATT, Annie; B: 1856; D: 1-16-1884; w/o L.W.
- WYLAND, A.H.D.; (no dates).
- WYLAND, Belle Keasey; B: 1844; D: 1928; w/o D.M.
- WYLAND, Christian J.; B: 1836, Elkhart Co., Ind.; D: 10-28-1897.
- WYLAND, Clarinda Stanley; B: 1849; D: 1933.
- WYLAND, D.M.; B: 1846; D: 1912.
- WYLAND, Helen Mary Thompson; B: 1831; D: 3-10-1896.
- WYLAND, I.P., "Father"; B: 1832; D: 1909.
- WYLAND, John J.; [no dates]; Ψ World War.
- WYLAND, Julia A.; B: 1828; D: 1914.
- WYLAND, Lenore Cullison; B: 1873; D: 1902.
- WYLAND, Mary H.; B: 1864; D: 1906; d/o I.W.
- WYLAND, Mollie; B: 1851; D: 1894.
- WYLAND, O.P.; B: 1855; D: 1923.

- WYLAND, Thos. Jefferson; B: 1849 Elkhart Co., Ind.; D: 1-27-1928; h/o Clara Osborn.
- WYLAND, W.W.; (no dates).
- WYLAND, William; B: 1830; D: 12-31-1911.
- YOUNCKIRST, Carl C.; B: 12-11-1888; D: 7-15-1917.
- YOUNG, G.A.; D: 9-20-1903.
- YOUNG, Mary A.; B: 1829; D: 12-29-1906; w/o Wm.
- YOUNG, Olive A.; B: 1853; D: 1-15-1928.
- YOUNG, Sadie Arline; B: 1905; D: 1918; d/o W.R. & Daisy Allen Young.
- YOUNG, William; B: 1827; D: 12-9-1914.
- ZIMMERMAN, Luella; B: 1878; D: 9-28-1881; d/o of J.J. & Leah.

Latter Day Saints (LDS) Cemetery

*The manuscript does not differentiate between two different cemeteries: **Latter Day Saints (LDS)** and **Reorganized Latter Day Saints (RLDS)**, so both are included as a single listing - if there was any designation, it is in this listing; otherwise all were shown as LDS.*

LDS (Church of Jesus Christ of Latter-Day Saints Cemetery).
Located northwest of Earling in Grove Township, Section 14. Cemetery is on the south side of 2300th Street west of Road M16.

RLDS (Reorganized Church of Jesus Christ of Latter Day Saints) Cemetery.
AKA: Gallands Grove Cemetery; RLDS Holcomb Memorial Cemetery; Abel Gallard Memorial Cemetery.
Located in Grove Township, Section 15. Located northwest of Earling. Cemetery is northwest of Earling. IA-37 West, to Street F16 east, to cemetery on the northon the north side of F16.

- ANDREWS, John M.; D: 4-12-1863; Age 32; Son of J.A. & A.N.
- BRYAN, John W.; D: 6-22-1902; Age 72.

- CHAMBERLIN, Herman O.; B: 1877; D: 12-7-1912.
- CLARK, Fannie C.; B: 1880; D: 1904; Dau W.W. & C.E.
- CLOTHIER, James W.; D: 10-2-1882; Age 27.
- COLE, Elizabeth; D: 1-30-1900; Age 77.
- COLE, Zachariah. B: 1826; D: 1-26-1880; h/o Elizabeth.
- CRANDALL, Daniel; B: 1808; D: 11-21-1883.
- CRANDALL, David C.; B: 1835; D: 1911.
- CRANDALL, Delila; B: 1811; D: 10-2-1902; w/o Patrick.
- CRANDALL, Lyman W.; B: 1840; D: 11-11-1919; Age 79.
- CRANDALL, Mary E.; B: 1849; D: 1917.
- CRANDALL, Maryette; D: 4-10-1878; Age 31; w/o L.
- CRANDALL, Parinth A.; B: 1817; D: 1-10-1885; Age 38 [68].
- CRANDALL, Patrick; B: 1819; D: 9-4-1894; Age 84.
- DARLING, Mary; D: 11-12-1879; Age 36; w/o D.
- FORD, Elizabeth; B: 1830; D: 11-4-1911; w/o Robt.
- FORD, Robert; B: 1830; D: 2-26-1908.
- FOUTS, Armah Giddeon; B: 2-29-1900; D: 6-16-1924.
- GOODALE, Joseph D.; D: 1-28-1891; Age 71.
- GREENWOOD, George; B: 1832; D: 7-17-1909.
- GREENWOOD, Mary; B: 1832; D: 5-3-1903; w/o Geo.
- HANKINS, Margaret; D: 3-4-1876; Age 73.
- HANSEN, Ingvert; B: 1836; D: 6-7-1889.
- HANSEN, Julia A.; B: 1860; D: 7-5-1934.
- HANSEN, Kate; B: 1837; D: 4-27-1915; w/o Ingvert.
- HAWLEY, Ann; B: 1830; D: 1886.
- HOLCOMB, Chauncey S.; B: 1844; D: 1-9-1917.
- HOLCOMB, Harmon C.; D: 2-25-1898; Age 59.
- HOLCOMB, Leslie L.; B: 1883; D: 1930.
- HOLCOMB, Mary L.; D: 8-21-1888; Age 35 w/o O.E.
- HOLCOMB, Menimento; B: 1848; D: 9-18-1894; w/o Chauncey.
- HOLCOMB, Nora A.; D: 7-22-1895; Age 40; w/o H.C.
- HOLCOMB, Oliver E.; B: 1841; D: 1914.
- HOLCOMB, Oliver E.; D: 8 Apr 1888; Age 71.
- HOLCOMB, Rosco; B: 1878; D: 5-20-1907.
- HOLCOMB, Sally; D: 10-25-1864; w/o O.E.
- HOMER, Eulia; D: 10-15-1884; Age 17.
- HOMER, Patience; D: 3-10-1867; Age 32; w/o Benj. T.

- HUNT, Alexander; D: 11-21-1873; Age 78; h/o Mary.
- HUNT, John B.; D: 10 Jun 1892; Age 59.
- HUNT, Mary; D: 4-12-1889; Age 91; w/o Alexander.
- INGRAM, Kezia; D: 2-5-1875; Age 74; w/o Sam'l.
- JENSEN, Inger; B: 1823; D: 6-25-51903; w/o R.P.
- JENSEN, L.; B: 1805; D: 8-18-1893.
- JONES, Nettie; D: 2-9-1895; Age 27; w/o J.H.
- LANE, Emily; D: 3-6-1874; Age 49; w/o J.K.
- McCORD, Ann J.; B: 1846; D: 1930.
- McCORD, Sibyl; D: 11-29-1900; Age 83; w/o Alex.
- McCORD, William; D: 1-24-1891; Age 48.
- PEARSALL, Harriet; B: 1847; D: 4-20-1916.
- PEARSALL, James; B: 1842; D: 12-28-1919.
- PERRY, Stephan; D: 12-29-1880; Age 92.
- PETERSON, Rasmus P.; B: 1837; D: 12-2-1908.
- PETT, John; D: 9-11-1913; Age 88; h/o Mary Ann.
- PETT, Mary Ann; D: 7-11-1892; Age 66; w/o John.
- RALPH, Jenkins; D: 2-24-1902; Age 46.
- REED, Mildred L.; B: 1885; D: 1917; w/o James A.
- ROLLS, John; D: 12-26-1877; Age 64.
- SHUMATE, Julia M.; D: 6-12-1886; Age 40.
- SHUMATE, N.; [no dates]; Ψ Co.A 30th Ia. Inf.
- SMITH, Henry; D: 8-15-1866; Age 55.
- SMITH, Laura E.; D: 1-2-1883; Age 20; w/o F.M.
- SMITH, S.F.; B: 1853; D: 1925.
- SMITH, Susanna Jex; B: 1820; D: 1912; w/o Henry.
- SPURGEON, Effie B.; B: 1878; D: 3-1-1914; w/o H. M.
- STERRETT, William; B: 1812; D: 4-25-1900.
- TALCOTT, Dora M.; B: 1877; D: 10-20-1903.
- WILLIAMSON, Chancy; B: 1823; D: 10-9-1898.
- WILLIAMSON, Elizabeth Jane; D: 10-25-1869; Age 38.
- WILLIAMSON, George; B: 1852; D: 1930.
- WILLIAMSON, Georgia; B: 1852; D: 1932; w/o of Geo.
- WILLIAMSON, Leanah; B: 1826; D: 2-7-1907.
- YOUNG, John; D: 10-30-1986; Age 75.
- YOUNG, Mary O.; D: 5-29-1865; d/o J. & P.

Lee Farm Cemetery

AKA: Howlett Cemetery.
Located east of Shelby in Fairview Township, Section 14. Cemetery is closer to Avoca (in Pottawattamie County): north on US 59 to 450th Street, then east to Mulberry Road to 400th Street

- CHAMBERS, Green B.; D: 5-25-1873; Age 78.
- CHRISTIANSEN, Anthon; D: 1880; Age 85.
- CHRISTIANSEN, Carrie; D: 1-27-1870; Age 37; w/o Anthon.
- HOWLET, Miram; D: 7-16-1875; Age 47; w/o Wm.

Lincoln Township Cemetery

AKA: Pleasant Ridge Cemetery.
Located in Harlan, Lincoln Township, Section 16. Cemetery is west of Harlan on IA-44.US-59, east of Hazel Road.

- BARE; Sarah Ann; D: 2-26-1879; Age 23; w/o Hiram.
- BITTLE, John; B: 10-13-1825; D: 4-3-1914.
- BITTLE, Ellen; B: 1832; D: 3-9-1911; w/o John.
- BOLAND, Eleanor; B: 1825; D: 9-16-1921.
- BOLAND, James; D: 9-19-1883; Age 52.
- BOTHWELL, John Brady; B: 1805; D: 1-4-1892; ψ Mexican War.
- BOYD, Elizabeth V.J.; D: 3-13-1882; Age 77; w/o John.
- BROWN, Chas. H.; B: 1862; D: 1-13-1888; Son of C. & E.
- BROWN, Eliza; B: 1817; D: 11-29-1892' w/o G.
- COMSTOCK, Margret J.; B: 1838; D: 5-29-1879.
- CRISPIN, Jessie; B: 1862; D: 8-22-1884; w/o G.R.
- DICKEY, Martha A.; B: 1836; D: 2-5-1904.
- DICKEY, Thomas J.; B: 1859; D: 1922/
- DICKEY, Thomas; D: 2-11-1887; Age 63.

- ERICKSON, Enoch N.; B: 1872; D: 12-13-1935; ψ Spanish-American.
- ERICKSON, Erick; B: 1843; D: 10-26-1929.
- ERICKSON, Henry; B: 1821; D: 6-27-1905.
- ERICKSON, O. J.; D: 4-18-1885; Age 21.
- ERICKSON, Olivia (or Olina); B: 1824; D: 11-10-1915; w/o Henry.
- ERICKSON, Willis M.; B: 1876; D: 4-28-1934.
- GROUSE, George; B: 1845; D: 2-6-1897.
- HILL, Anna M.; B; 1857; D: 9-16-1898.
- JENSEN, Cora; B: 1797; D: 1-15-1861.
- JENSEN, Jens; D: 5-16-1874; Age 31.
- JOHNSON, Louisa; D: 2-11-1885; Age 61; w/o M.
- JUSTICE, John; B: 1832; D: 9-1-1916.
- JUSTICE, Marhareta [Margareta?]; D: 3-24-1881; Age 53; w/o John.
- KENNEY, Caroline; B: 1852; D: 1-16-1877; w/o R.
- KOHL, Hannah; D: 5-1-1887; Age 68; w/o Wm.
- KOHL, William; D: 6-14-1901; Age 84.
- LOWN, Mary E.; B: 4-11-1883; Age 28; d/o E & D Gries.
- McCULLOUGH, Elizabeth; B: 1868; D: 1913.
- MILLER, Ann Hillis; B: 1806; D: 6-6-1891.
- MITCHELL, Marion H.; B: 1832.
- MYRTNE, Andrew S.; B: 1841; D: 1924.
- MYRTNE, Christine; B: 1839; D: 1913; w/o A.S.
- NELSON, Maria; D: 12-14-1898; Age 75; w/o Otto.
- NELSON, Otto; D: 5-13-1904; Age 74.
- OLSEN, Olivia; D: 2-17-1893; Age 23.
- QUASS, Jenni R.; B: 1863; D: 1-20-1885; w/o L.C.
- SEITEL, Lena; D: 8-18-1879; Age 25; d/o Frank & Elizabeth.
- TAYLOR, G.E.; B: 1844; D: 1911.
- TAYLOR. Amanda L.; D: 4-27-1900; Age 51; w/o G.E.
- TRIERWEILER, Elizabeth; B: 1842; D: 7-21-1886.
- TRIERWEILER, Peter; B: 1838; D: 11-11-1900.
- WEAVER, Sarah J.; B: 1858; D: 2-18-1890; w/o S.N.
- WILSON, Andrew A.; D: 11-20-1887; Age 44.
- WINDER, Henry; B: 1816; D: 1-31-1889.
- WINDER, Jane; B: 1813; D: 3-8-1896.

Merrills Grove Cemetery

Located in Fiscus in Polk Township, Section 26. Cemetery is east of Kirkman, south of County Road F32, on the west side of Wildwood Road.

- CHRISTENSEN, ---; B: 1897; D: 1919
- HANSEN, Anne Marie; B: 1866; D: 1927.
- HANSON, Chas. A.; B: 1887; D: 12-23-1928.
- HANSON, Dora M.; B: 1874; D: 11-14-1919.
- JACOBSEN, C.F.; B; 1868; D: 1918.
- JACOBSEN, M.M.; B: 1870; D: 1927.
- JACOBSEN, Norman M.; B: 1895; D: 1923.
- JENSEN, Harvey; B: 1857; D: 1925.
- JENSEN, Kjerstine; B: 1842; D: 1918; w/o Nels P.
- JENSEN, Mary; B: 1876; D: 1930.
- JENSEN, Nels P.; B: 1941.
- JENSEN, Roy A.; B: 1916; D: 1932.
- MICHAELSON, Pauline; B: 1838; D: 1929.
- NELSON, Chris; B: 1866, Denmark; D: 2-12-1966.
- NELSON. Anna; B: 1878; D: 1902.
- NIELSEN, Emma E. Larson; B: 1885; D: 6-14-1912; w/o Andrew.
- NIELSEN, K.N.; B: 1863; D: 1935.
- NIELSEN, Richard; D: 1922; s/o R.& C.
- PEDERSEN; Jens P.; B: 1860; D: 1922.
- PETERSEN, Anna H.; B: 1853; D: 1908.
- PETERSEN, Anna M.; B: 1870; D: 1938.
- PETERSEN, Martin; B: 1865; D: 1899.
- PETERSEN, Peter S.; B: 1852; D: 1923.
- SCOTT, Jansena Petra; B: 1866; D: 3-22-1902.
- WILLADSEN, Christiana; B: 1885; D: 11-10-1905; d/o L. & M.
- WILLADSEN, Lars; B: 1838; D: 1916.

Monroe Township Cemetery

AKA: Monroe United Methodist Church Cemetery.
Located southeast of Harlan in Monroe Township, Section 25.
Cemetery is east of US-59, south of Rd M47 on Umbrella Road.

- ANDERSON, Emil N.; B: 1876, Roscobel, WI; D: 3-1-1923; Res. Corley, Ia.; h/o Lena Ehmke.
- PORTER, Robert; B: 1832, England; D: 1-2-1918; Age 85; Shelby Co. Reporter, Jan, 1918 (no burial record).

Oak Hill Cemetery

Located just south of Irwin in Jefferson Township, Section 31.
Cemetery is east of Front Street/Road M47.

- #BARRETT, Bruce Banner; D: 7-21-1936; Age 50; Burial Permit (copy in DAR transcription)
- CARSEN, Eli Eldridge; B: 1860, Jasper Co., Ia.; D: 2-17-1933, Rockwell; h/o Delana Farrell; Burial Record, Irwin, Shelby Co.
- ZIMMER, Michael; B: 2-14-1836, Pittsburg[h], Pa.; D: 3-14-1917, Irving; Ψ Co.B 160th reg, Ohio nat'l guards.

Poplar Cemetery

[Sometimes recorded as Popular Cemetery]
Located south of Irwin in Polk Township, Section 36. Cemetery is east of Rd M47, south of 1700th Street.

- ALBERTSEN, Anna; B: 10-4-1887; D: 10-7-1911; w/o Hans.
- CHRISTENSEN, Emil; B: 1895; D: 5-14-1911.
- CHRISTOFFERSEN, Karen; B: 1859; D: 1932.
- JOHNSON, Anna; B: 1888; D: 11-9-1921.
- JOHNSON, Mary Lou; (no dates).
- JOHNSON, Samuel; B: 1849; D: 1-15-1918.
- NIELSEN, Johannes; B: 1822; D: 2-7-1909.

- OTZN, Paul; B: 1854; D: 1915.
- RASSMUSSEN, Knud; B: 1834; D: 1919.
- WOLTERS, Mads R.; B: 1872; D: 1922.

Plus 8 unmarked graves noted.

Red Line Cemetery

Located north of Jacksonville in Polk Township, Section 21. Cemetery is on the west side of County Road M56 north of Jacksonville.

- BARTELSON, John; (no dates).
- BARTELSON, Samuel; B: 1883; D: 3-4-1905.
- BERGER, William F.; B: 1870; D: 8-31-1931.
- BOLMAN, W.H.; B: 1869; D: 1933.
- BURGER, Sarah; (no dates); w/o Zachariah.
- BURGER, Zachariah; B: 10-22-1856; D: 12-6-1912.
- DAHLOF, Samuel; D: 9-25-1909; Age 87.
- DENT, Loretta D.; B: 1852; D: 1932.
- DENT, William H.; B: 1849; D: 1926.
- DOWELL, W.T.; D: 12-16-1891; Age 35.
- ELZY, Charles; [no dates].
- ELZY, Rosannah; B: 1858; D: 1922.
- FISCUS, --; (no dates).
- FISCUS, Chas. Allyn; B: 1894; D: Jan 1918; ψ World War.
- FISCUS, Deene; (no dates).
- FISCUS, Dillie; (no dates); w/o Louis.
- FISCUS, Elmer; D: 1938; Age 30.
- FISCUS, Walter; D: abt 1917; Age 20.
- FISCUS, Willis; (no dates).
- GAER, Almarion; B: 1830; D: 6-17-1915; h/o Nancy.
- GAER, Clara; B: 1888; D: 1926.
- GAER, Lurana; D: 1-16-1904; Age 76.
- GAER, Nancy; B: 1831; D: 12-23-1891; w/o Almerion.
- GAER, Philip M.; B: 1853; D: 1-26-1901.
- GAER, Shelton; B: 1820; D: 3-10-1897.

- GAER, William C.; D: 11-11-1910.
- GEAR, Cavender; (no dates).
- GEAR, Cavender; B: 1809; D: 1-27-1896.
- GEAR, Frank; (no dates).
- GEAR, Rebecca; (no dates); w/o Umri.
- GEAR, Umri; (no dates).
- GEAR, Viola; (no dates); w/o Cavender.
- GREEN, Frances O.; B: 1855; D: 1935.
- GREEN, Ida A.; D: 8-9-1896; Age 39; w/o Newton.
- GREEN, Newton; B: 1851; D: 1906.
- HON, Jessee; B: 1827; D: 1-21-1933.
- HON, Nelson; B: 1851; D: 2-2-1935.
- KAUFFMAN, Fannie L.; B: 1860; D: 1937.
- MARTINDALE, Henry C.; B: 1852; D: 8-1-1895.
- MICHAELSON, John; Age 59[54?].
- MICHAELSON, Lars; D: 12-20-1904; Age 70.
- MILLER, Charles A.; B: 1857; D: 4-22-1934.
- MILLER, Layella; B: 11-26-1863.
- MILLER, Noah; D: 9-28-1907; Age 76.
- MILLER, Rebecca; D: 7-11-1906; Age 72; w/o Noah.
- NUGENT, Robt. Judson; D: 5-1-1918; Age 23.
- ROBERTS, Will E.; D: 8-15-1935; Age 61.
- SMITH, Jesse W.; B: 1832; D: 1916.
- SMITH, Almira; B: 1843; D: 1918; w/o Jesse.
- SNYDER, Edith A.; B: 1893; D: 1918.
- STEVENS, Henry L.; B: 1870; D: 5-17-1915.
- TAGUE, Eliza; B: 1843; D: 1928.
- TAGUE, Geo. W.; B: 1842; D: 1898.
- TOWNSEND, Arthur C.; (no dates).
- WALDO, Clementine E.; B: 1856; D: 1924.
- WALDO, Robert; B: 1857; D: 1934.

Rose Hill Cemetery

AKA: Kirkman Cemetery.
Located northwest of Kirkman in Douglas Township, Section 10.
Cemetery is west of Washington Street on the south side of County
Road F32.

- ABRELL, Jacob; D: 5-8-1914; Age 29.
- ADAMS, Charles E.; D: 2-27-1905; Age 18.
- ADAMS, Mary Jane; D: 1925; Age 23.
- ADAMS, William R.; D: 3-20-1936; Age 72.
- AMES, D.D.; B: 1835; D: 5-12-1893.
- AMES, Delacie A. Shafer; D: 11-15-1899; Age 24; w/o W.W.
- AMES, Hannah; B: 1862; D: 1-21-1928.
- AMES, Mulissie; B: 1863; D:3-24-1900; w/o G.F.
- ANDERSON, Marion N.; D: 1-24-1907; s/o R. & A.
- BARBER, J.K.; B: 1838; D: 1921.
- BARBER, Joseph L.; B; 1868; D: 4-20-1933.
- BARBER, Sarah E. B: 1837; D: 1914; w/o J.K.
- BARTON, Adolphus; B: 1853; D: 1931.
- BARTON, Leverett; B: 1865; D: 3-24-1902.
- BARTON, Merills; B: 1823; D: 4-11-1905.
- BARTON, Palona C.; B: 1820; D: 2-3-1896; w/o Merills.
- BARTON, Phebe; B: 1868; D: 12-25-1923; w/o Leverett.
- BAUGHMAN, Clarence; D: 4-10-1900; Age 49.
- BAUGHMAN, Maudee; (no dates).
- BAUGHMAN, Sam; B: 1883; D: 1930.
- BEAVER, Mary L.; B: 1870; D: 6-28-1928.
- BIRD, John H.; B: 1880; D: 3-8-1916.
- BIRD, Mary; B: 1854; D: 8-8-1904; w/o S. L.
- BLAINE, Eliza J.; B: 1844; D: 1911; w/o Lewis.
- BLAINE, Lewis Wm.; B: 1841; D: 1-22-1907; ψ Co.D 47th Pa. Vols.
- BLAINE, Sophia; B: 1845; D: 1923.
- BOYD, James R.; B: 1836; D: 1913.
- BOYD, Valeria A.; B: 1841; D: 1906.
- BROWN, B.F.; B: 1818, Maine; D: 7-15-1918; Wives: Jane Kent; Susan Beckworth & Mary Stockton.

- CAMPBELL, Juliette Kibby; B: 1845; D: 1927.
- CARTER, Lee; B: 1854; D: 3-22-1930.
- CARTER, Mary J.; B: 1858; D: 12-3-1913; w/o Lee.
- CASTEEL, John S.; D: 3-22-1906; Age 29; Son of John & Cyrena.
- CROFT, Alice; B: 1860; D: 2-16-1938.
- CROFT, George S.; B: 1845; D: 4-21-1914.
- CROFT, Nathan C.; D: 4-10-1897; Age 52.
- CROFT, Roy Burnell; B: 1885; D: 2-16-1917; s/o Geo. & Alice.
- CURTIS, Laura E.; B: 1877; D: 1-31-1904; w/o Frank A.
- DeFORD, Elijah; B: 1815; D: 2-21-1907.
- DeFORD, Susan; B: 1818; D: 2-12-1907; w/o Elijah.
- DeFORD, William A.; B: 1848; D: 9-28-1909.
- EGGLESTON, Alda Veslan; B: 1906; D: 1936; w/o Everett.
- ERICKSON, John; B: 1869; D: 1922.
- ERICKSON, Ray Gailen; B: 1915; D: 1936; s/o J & E.
- FAIRCHILD, "Daughter"; B: 1871; D: 7-29-1937; Age 66.
- FAIRCHILD, "Father"; B: 5-30-1841; D: 6-6-1934.
- FAIRCHILD, "Mother"; B: 1849; D: 1-27-1888.
- FERGUSON, Geo. T.; B: 1854.
- FERGUSON, Lucelia Rummel; B: 1854; D: 3-5-1910; w/o Geo.
- FOUNTAIN, Jesse H.; B: 1888; D: 1905; s/o P. & E.A.
- FOUNTAIN, Pierson; B: 1838; D: 1910; ψ Co. D 55th Mass. Inf.
- GARST, Anna Agnes; B: 1869; D: 1921.
- GARST, Joseph Morris; B: 1867; D: 1932.
- GARTON, Barbara; B: 1878; D: 7-12-1916; w/o W.L.
- GRACE, John; B: 1871; D: 1937.
- GRAHAM, H.W.; B:1871; D: 8-18-1895.
- HAMDORF, Mary Vogy; D: 6-8-1891; Age 42; w/o Henry.
- HARRIS, Anna A.; D: [8]-23-1904; Age 38; w/o S.J.
- HARRIS, V.J.; B: 1892; D: 1936; h/o Tina.
- HICKS, Catharine L.; B: 1805; D: 1894.
- HILBERT, Johannes H.; B: 1867; D: 1916.
- HMNDORF, Henry H.; D: 11-5-1925.
- JENSEN. Elmer Anton; D: 1-6-1916; s/o Chris & Emma.
- JOHNSON, Martha E.; B: 1849; D: 1930; w/o Chas. A.
- JOHNSON, Mary A.; B: 1830; D: 1916; w/o Washington A.
- JOHNSON, Peter I.; B: 1843; D: 3-18-1926.

- JOHNSON, Washington A.; B: 1819; D: 1917.
- KIBBY, Charles; D: 2-15-1901; Age 62.
- KIBBY, Ernest S.; D: 7-3-1892; Age 27; s/o G. & J.
- KIBBY, George; D: 9-22-1881; Age 63.
- KIBBY, Helen; B: 1882; D: 1926.
- KIBBY, V.M.; B: 1869; D: 1925.
- KIMBALL, Chas. J.; D: 1-8-1903; Age 85.
- KIMBALL, Sarah; D: 3-12-1918; Age 91; w/o Chas. J.
- KNOUSE, Chas. W.; D: 2-22-1902; Age 29.
- KNOUSE, Joseph; B: 2-5-1893; D: 12-17-1918.
- KOBS, William; B: 1875; D: 1912.
- LEWIS, J.G.; B: 10-24-1880; D: 2-27-1927.
- LEWIS, Clarence R.; B: 1879; D: 1927.
- LEWIS, E.M.; B: 1847; D: 3-16-1917.
- LEWIS, Grace Evelyn; B: 1879; D: 1928.
- LEWIS, Grace; B: 1854; D: 8-20-1908; w/o E.M.
- LEWIS, Harriet T.; B: 1886; D: 1936.
- MARCO, Naomi Odeet; D: 12-4-1925; d/o E.J. & Hazel.
- MARSHALL, Fay R.; B: 1855; D: 1918.
- McDOWELL, E. Jane; D: 6-11-1919; Age 73.
- McDOWELL, Elizabeth; B: 1860; D: 1928.
- McDOWELL, F.M.; B: 1841; D: 1923.
- McDOWELL, John; B: 1852; D: 1906.
- McDOWELL, Luke; D: 7-20-1911; Age 64.
- McDOWELL, William P.; B: 1868; D: 4-4-1927.
- McGEE, Earl; B: 1889; D: 1928.
- MILES, John D.; B: 1859; D: 1924.
- MILES, John Wilson; D: 7-29-1919; ψ World War.
- MITCHELL, Lucinda E.; D: 1-21-1911; w/o Thos.
- MITCHELL, Thomas; D: 8-15-1911; Age 35.
- MOLER, Thomas M.; D: 5-24-1925; Age 23.
- MUCKLER, Francis C.; B: 1835; D: 3-13-1898.
- NEWHOUSE, Aner; D: 7-3-1898; w/o Geo.
- NEWHOUSE, George; B: 1833; D: 1915.
- NICHOLS, Caroline S.; B: 1828; D: 12-1-1905.
- NICHOLS, Humphrey E.; B: 1830; D: 11-26-1926.
- OLESON, Adtri; B: 1809; D: 2-24-1905.

- OLSON, Barry; B: 1816; D: 4-29-1886.
- OLSON, Frank; B: 1894; D: 1928.
- OLSON, Henry A.; B: 1882; D: 9-4-1919.
- OLSON, Ole B.; B: 1851; D: 3-31-1930.
- OLSON, Stena; D: 3-19-1885; Age 33; w/o T.B.
- OLSON, Tobias B.; D: 9-11-1899; Age 51.
- OTTAWAY, Almira Adkins; B: 1829; D: 12-19-1911; w/o Horace.
- OTTAWAY, Horace; B: 1815; D: 1-21-1897.
- PALMER, H.E.; B: 1836; D: 6-2-1903.
- PALMER, W.O.; B: 1866; D: 12-22-1893.
- PAUSTIAN, Christ; B: 1848; D: 6-2-1897.
- PAUSTIAN, Rica; B: 1850; D: 7-24-1932.
- PENCE, Harry R.; B: 1906; D: 1931.
- POTTER, Henry C.; B: 1853; D: 1919.
- PRATT, Laura B.; D: 7-30-1914; Age 28; w/o Roy.
- PULVER, Harmon; D: 1-4-1909; Age 71.
- PULVER, Ida V.; B: 1857; D: 1905.
- PULVER, Permelia; B: 1840; D: 1917.
- RANK, Anna; B: 1832; D: 1921; w/o Jonathan.
- RANK, Charles H.; B: 1864; D: 1933.
- RANK, Jonathan; B: 1831; D: 1916.
- RASSMUSSEN, Kersten; B: 1834; D: 1914; w/o Knud.
- RONFELDT, Chas.; B: 1872; D: 1928.
- RUMMEL, Martin Kline; D: 11-2-1897; Age 69.
- RUMMEL, Rebecca Fisher; D: 3-7-1885; Age 55; w/o M.K.
- SCHREINER, Eden C.; B: 1902; D: 1929.
- SEVERNS, Kate R.; B: 1882; D: 1933.
- SHEARMAN, Emma J.; B: 1870; D: 1926.
- SHEELEY, Alta B.; B: 1870; D: 12-8-1899; w/o L.
- SLATES, Chas. H.; B: 1876.
- SLATES, Ida L.; B: 1850; D: 1920.
- SLATES, John; D: 3-22-1881; Age 21; s/o S & L.
- SLATES, Lucretia; D: 11-15-1881; Age 51; 1st w/o Sam'l.
- SLATES, Richard; B: 1881; D: 1897.
- SLATES, Samuel; B: 1828; D: 1-8-1901.
- SLATES, Sarah J.; B: 1833; D: 1913; 2d w/o Sam'l.
- SLICK, Lela M.; B: 1864; D: 8-5-1913.

- STEEN, Sarah A.; B: 1850; D: 1923.
- STEEN, Robert; D: 7-15-1895; Age 51.
- STOLLEY, John D.; D: 10-3-1907.
- STOLLEY, Katherine; B: 1851; D: 11-13-1893.
- STORY, Francis M.; D: 9-28-1905; Age 72.
- STORY, Hannah E.; D: 5-15-1906; Age 62; w/o F.M.
- SUNDERLAND, Clara E.; B: 1866; D: 1925.
- SUNDERLAND, William L.; B: 1862; D: 3-14-1906.
- THOMAS, Absalom; B: 1841; D: 1908; Ψ 8th O. Art. & 87th O. Inf.
- THOMAS, Louisa; D: 8-8-1912; Age 58; w/o Geo.
- THOMAS, Lucinda; B: 1839; D: 1885; w/o A.
- TUCKER, Elmer B.; B: 1850; D: 1938.
- WESTROPE, Orville D.; D: 3-28-1898; Age 37.
- WESTROPE, Sarah A.; D: 4-24-1896; Age 63; w/o T.R.
- WESTROPE, Thomas R.; D: 6-14-1902;
- WILSON, Lucy L.; B: 1869; D: 1-16-1901; w/o Eli.
- WILSON, Sophia; B: 1829; D: 1917.
- WOODS, Anna N.; D: 3-25-1904; Age 32; w/o James   .
- WOODS, James; B: 1868; D: 1923.
- WOODS, Nellie I.; D: 1-4-1894; Age 20; d/o M.H. & E.C.
- YOST, Alida J.; D: 1-16-1899; Age 47; d/o T.F.
- YOST, Thos. F.; B: 1845; D: 7-25-1930; Ψ Co.C 53rd Ill. Inf.

Shelby Cemetery

Located south of Shelby in Shelby Township, Section 33. Cemetery is west off East Street.

- #ALBERTUS, Gustavus A.; B: 1867, Sioux City, Wis.; D: 11-24-1938, Avoca; h/o Anna M. Bickels; Source: Journal Herald 12-1-1938.
- BENFER, Lewis Albert; B: 1847, Ashtabula, O; D: 7-3-1920; h/o Erma Thomp[son?]; Avoca Journal Herald, 7-15-1920.
- BICKELS, John Wm.; B: 1874, Shelby Co., Ia.; D: 5-12-1925, Shelby, Ia.; Wife Johanna; Avoca Journal Herald, 5-27-1925.

- BRUGGE, John; D: 2-25-1939; Age 50; Wife Hazel; Res. Persia.
- BURMEISTER. Wm. L.; D: 8-28-1938; Age 59, In Council Bluffs, Ia.; Son of Theodore & Doris; Informant Nellie Ganble, Oersie [Persia?], Iowa.
- CLAPP, E.C.; B: 1851, Brooklyn, NY; D: 6-11-1913, Los Angeles, Calif.; h/o Leila Nordoff.
- CLAUSSEN, John Henry; B: 1857, Germany; D: 1-13-1919, Avoca; h/o Anna Schadebrodt; Avoca Journal-Herald, 1-23-1919.
- COLLINS, Ed Addison; B: 1852, Galena, Il.; D: 11-19-1922; h/o Elizabeth Graybill.
- DOLLEN, Hannes J.; B: 1874, Germany; D: 5-6-1937; [Wife Kate A. Stoker]; Res near Persia.
- GREGERSON, Nicolai Peter; B: 1873, Germany; D: 6-26-1937; h/o Emma Stendor.
- HAGEN, Julius H.; D: 7-8-1922; Age 43; h/o Alvina [P.?] Matthiesen.
- HOLDORF, Charles; B: 1861, Clinton Co., Ia; D: 10-28-1933, Avoca Ia.; (wife Sophie Schmidt); s/o Fred'k & Johanna.
- ICKES, Leroy; B: 1882, Wash.Twp.; D: 9-6-1921; h/o Lilly Scherfler.
- JOHNSON, John C.; B: 1850, Denmark; D: 2-19-1938; h/o Henrietta Neilsen.
- LATENDORF, Ernest W.; B: 1887, Davenport, Ia.; D: 3-1-1919, [Glenns Ferry, Idaho]; h/o Lydia Schultz; Burial record.
- SUTTON, John Harvey; B: 1859, Cococton [Coshocton] Co, O.; D: 10-6-1922; h/o Rhoda E. Forester.
- TATMAN, Chas. M.; B: 1850, Miam[i] Co., O.; D: 7-3-1916; h/o Mary E. Reder.
- TERRILL, Gordon; D: 3-14-1938; Age 59; h/o Effie; s/o David & Margaret.
- THORNBURG, H.V.; D: 7-14-1928.
- WEST, Leonard Tate; B: 10-9-1895, Shelby; D: 7-1-1920, [?]ils [Miles?] City, Mont.; s/o Elza & Lucy; Avoca Journal Herald, 7-10-1920.

Slates Cemetery

Located in Earling in Union Township, Section 32. Cemetery is east of Washington Street, on County Road 32, at Peach Road.

- HAYES, Catherine; D: May 1877; w/o Chas.

St. Boniface Cemetery

AKA: Westphalia Cemetery.
Located north of Westphalia in Westphalia Township, Section 21. Cemetery is west of 2nd Street, at Duren Street, job east, then north, cemetery is west of Sunrise Drive.

- McGUELLEN [McQUILLEN], Bernard; B: 1825, Ireland; D: 1-3-1901; h/o Mary Sweeney; Burial record Westphalia, Ia.; Res. Harlan, Ia.
- McQUILLAN [McQUILLEN?], Patrick Wm.; B: 1866, Fayette Co. Ia.; D: 8-7-1891; Westphalia Cemetery; Guthrie newspaper, 2-20-1891.

St. Joseph Cemetery

Located on the north edge of Earling, north of 3rd Street, on the east side of Rd M16.

- HEESE, Henry; D: 5-21-1936, Council Bluffs, Ia.; Burial record.
- HEESE, John; D: 12-28-1938; Age 50; Burial record.
- MILLER, M.A.; B: 1878, Cascade, Ia.; D: 2-24-1931, Earling, Ia.; h/o Gertrude Cross; Buried there Catholic cem.
- STEPHANY, S.F.; D: 3-27-1938; Age 64; s/o John & Agnes; h/o Kate.

St. Mary's (Panama) Cemetery

Located in Panama in Washington Township, Section 22. Cemetery is at Main Street and North 2nd Street.

- BEHRENDT, Albert; B: 1871; D: 1934.
- BEHRENDT, Joseph; B: 1852; D: 5-28-1929.
- BEHRENDT, Mary; B: 1853; D: 9-24-1933; w/o Joseph.
- BEHRENDT, Rosalia; B: 1845; D: 3-25-1914; w/o Wm. (Wilhelm?).
- BEHRENDT, Wilhelm; B: 1838; D: 1-16-1911.
- BLUM, Helen A.; (no dates).
- BLUM, Katharine; B: 1864; D: 3-20-1928; w/o Michael.
- BLUM, Mary A.; (no dates).
- BUCKLEY, Catherine; B: 1880; D: 1921.
- BUCKLEY, Gertrude; B: 1905; D: 1930.
- BUCKLEY, James; B: 1863; D: 1938.
- BUCKLEY, John; B: 1866; D: 1927.
- BUCKLEY, Mary; B: 1834; D: 1902.
- BUCKLEY, Robert P.; (no dates).
- BUCKLEY, Thomas; B: 1871; D: 1896.
- BUCKLEY, Thomas; B: 1901; D: 1918.
- BUCKLEY, Timothy Jr.; B: 1868; D: 1926.
- BUCKLEY, Timothy; B: 1831; D: 1918; ψ GAR marker.
- CAREY, Mary A. Sullivan; B: 1889; D: 5-23-1917; w/o John D.
- CARROLL, John S.; B: 1861; D: 1922.
- CARROLL, Marion J. (male); D: Jan. 11, 1900; Age 64.
- CARROLL, Mary E.; B: 1863; D: 1920.
- CARROLL, Samuel; B: 1831; D: 6-17-1900.
- CARROLL, Teresa Scallon; B: 1832; D: 2-1-1896.
- CHASE, Anne; (no dates).
- CHASE, Henry N.; (no dates).
- COOPER, Mary; B: 1821; D: 2-27-1904.
- CROGHAN, Elizabeth; B: 1861; D: 1956.
- CROGHAN, Mary; D: 2-17-1906; Age 74; w/o Owen.
- CROGHAN, Owen; D: 6-8-1901; Age 70.
- DOMINSSE, --; B: 1866; D: 1923.
- DOWNEY, Martha L.; B: 1-16-1894; D: 6-24-1936.

- ENGEL, Irene; [no dates].
- ENGEL, Michael; B: 1877; D: 1935.
- FLYNN, "Father"; B: 1824; D: 1904.
- FLYNN, "Mother"; B: 1832; D: 1911; with father?
- FLYNN, Catherine; B: 1873; D: 1896.
- FLYNN, Margaret; B: 1873; D: 1934.
- FLYNN, Mary; B: 1866; D: 1920.
- FLYNN, Michael; B: 1871; D: 1934.
- FLYNN, Patrick; D: 3-11-1904; Age 80.
- FLYNN, William; B: 1868; D: 1910.
- GEIGER, Katherine; (no dates).
- GOESER, Mary E.; B: 1879; D: 1921; w/o Nick.
- GOETZ, Agnes; (no dates).
- GROSS, Mary Ann; B: 1862; D: 11-10-1908; w/o J.
- HANSEN, Frances; (no dates).
- HOFFMAN, Eva; (no dates); w/o W.
- HOFFMAN, Frederick; B: 1868; D: 12-13-1917.
- HOFFMAN, Lambert; B: 1908; D: 1928.
- HOFFMAN, Nicholas; (no dates).
- KAUFFMAN, Peter; B: 1873; D: 1938.
- KEANE, Julia; B: 1857; D: 1929.
- KEANE, Thomas; B: 1863; D: 1936
- KOCH, Clara; (no dates).
- KOCH, H. Joseph; (no dates).
- KOCH, Natalia K.; (no dates).
- KWAKISZESKI, Martin J.; B: 1855; D: 1937.
- KWAKISZESKI, Mary A.; B: 1856; D: 1933; w/o Martin .
- LAHR, Genevera; B: 1834; D: 11-10-1904; w/o Henry.
- LAHR, Henry; B: 1825; D: 4-27-1898.
- LUZ, J.P.; B: 1838; D: 5-4-1911.
- MAGES, Martin; (no dates).
- MAHLBERG, Gertrude; B: 1866; D: 1927; w/o Peter.
- MAHLBERG, Margaret; B: 1853; D: 9-24-1911; w/o Thos.
- MANHART, Catherine; B: 1859; D: 2-17-1930.
- MANHART, Lawrence; B: 1853; D: 11-23-1907.
- MANION, Bridget; B: 1847; D: 5-8-1927.
- MANION, Mary M.; B: 1870; D: 1-28-1914.

- MANION, Michael; B: 1831; D: 5-20-1909.
- McALLISTER, Bernard; B: 1840; D: 1920.
- McALLISTER, Catherine; B: 1853; D: 1920.
- MICHELS, Delmer; (no dates).
- MICHELS, Gertrude; B: 1850; D: 1924; w/o Peter.
- MICHELS, Peter; B: 1838; D: 1918.
- MISCHE, Apollonia; B: 1857; D: 1-8-1925; w/o John.
- MISCHE, Michael; B: 1845; D: 5-4-1925.
- MITCHELL, Julia A. B: 1944; w/o M.H.
- MORRIS, Mary; (no dates).
- MUELL, Anna M.; B: 1864; D: 1915; w/o John.
- MUELL, Elnore; D: 1905.
- MUELLER, Amalia; B: 1854; D: 7-30-1904; w/o Michael.
- OHLINGER, Clara A.; B: 1893; D: 1936; w/o Michael.
- OPPOLD, Casper A.; B: 1847; D: 8-15-1938.
- OPPOLD, Margaret; B: 1850; D: 10-22-1930.
- OPPOLD, Nelle; B: 1882; D: 1920.
- PIMPLE, Fred'k.; B: 1851; D: 7-2-1924.
- POTTER, Henry M.; B: 1865; D: 1937.
- QUEENEY, Ellen; B: 1831; D: 1908.
- QUEENEY, James; D: 2-15-1912; Age 87.
- QUEENEY, John M.; B: 1860; D: 1924.
- QUEENEY, Maria; B: 1861; D: 8-6-1906; w/o John M.
- QUEENEY, William; B: 1862; D: 9-2-1937.
- RATIGAN, Michael; B: 1875; D: 1917.
- REINIG, Agnes; B: 1867; D: 1935.
- ROSENTHAL, Clara Domin[i]sse; B: 1892; D: 1919; w/o Joseph.
- SCHAFER, Theresia; B: 1850; D: 1-4-1918.
- SCHOEMANN, Barbara; B: 1874; D: 1-13-1919; w/o Nikolas.
- SCHOEMANN, Marie; B: 1907; D: 5-30-1935.
- SCHOMER, Anna; D: 9-22-1898; Age 20; d/o J. & N.
- SCHOMER, Catharine; B: 1859; D: 1938; w/o Jacob.
- SCHOMER, Jacob; B: 1849; D: 1922.
- SCHUTTE, Henry E.; (no dates).
- SCHWERY, Godfrey; B: 1835; D: 2-12-1914
- THEISEN, Gertrude; B: 1848; D: 4-26-1933; w/o John.
- THEISEN, John; B: 1849; D: 12-12-1928.

- THIELEN, Magdalena; B: 1856; D: 1937; w/o John Sr.
- THILLEN, Barbara; B: 1836; D: 7-19-1923.
- THILLEN, Catherine; B: 1879; D: 1936.
- WILLMAS, Marcella A.; B: 1911; D: 1932.
- WINGERT, Eva; B: 1846; D: 12-30-1913; w/o Peter.
- WINGERT, Martha; B: 2-8-1889; D: 3-22-1930.
- WINGERT, Peter; B: 1831; D: 7-18-1912.
- WINGERT, Peter; B: 1869; D: 12-1-1933.
- ZIMMERMAN, Joseph; B: 1858; D: 1926.
- ZIMMERMAN, Luella; B: 1878; D: 9-28-1881; d/o of J.J. & Leah.
- ZIMMERMAN, Richard; B: 1893; D: 1935.

St. Mary's (Portsmouth) Cemetery

Located in Portsmouth, Cass Township, Section 17. Cemetery is to the west of St. Mary's Catholic Church, north of 3rd Avenue and west of 4th Street.

- BAKER, George; D: Sept. 6, 1901; Age 64.
- BAXTER, "Father"; B: 1849; D: 1906.
- BAXTER, "Mother"; B: 1855; D: 1937.
- BENDON, Annastasia; B: 1845; D: 1934; w/o Simon.
- BENDON, D.A.; B: 1-19-1841; D: 6-14-1922.
- BENDON, Simon; B: 1843; D: 1928; ψ Co.K 225 Pa. Vols.
- BOOK, Anna; B: 1873; D: 3-28-1913; w/o Wm.
- BRODERICK, Michael A.; B: 1834; D: 1-3-1904.
- BROWN, Margaret; B: 1842; D: 8-20-1914.
- BROWN, William; (no dates).
- BUMAN, Joseph E.; B: 1882; D: 1916.
- BUMAN, Rose E.; (no dates).
- BURNS, Elizabeth; B: 1851; D: 1-21-1880; w/o Wm.
- BURNS, William; B: 3-16-1840; D: 1-12-1919.
- CAREY, John Clark; B: 1835; D: 11-27-1929.
- CAREY, Julia A.; B: 5-1-1848; D: 10-19-1919.
- CAREY, Mamie; [no dates].
- COSGROVE, James; D. 1-21-1887; Age 28; s/o T. & M.

- COSGROVE, Mary; B: 1833; D: 1893; w/o Thomas.
- COSGROVE, Thomas; B: 1828; D: 1911.
- COUGHLIN, Biddy; (no dates).
- COUGHLIN, Ellen; D: 1-10-1887.
- COUGHLIN, Margaret; (no dates).
- COUGHLIN, Margie; D: 11-30-1889; Age 20; d/o T & [?].
- COUGHLIN, Mary; B: 1846; D: 11-17-1888; w/o Patrick.
- COUGHLIN, Mathew; B: 1863; D: 3-29-1922.
- COUGHLIN, Patrick; B: 1835; D: 4-24-1915.
- COUGHLIN, Thomas; (no dates).
- DAEGES, Michael; B: 1837; D: 3-2-1911.
- DESMANN, Martin; B: 1834; D: 6-29-1911.
- DESMANN, Rosalga; B: 1838; D: 4-21-1906.
- DOWNEY, Francese; B: 1862; D: 1920.
- DOWNEY, Henry H.; D: 4-28-1903; Age 33.
- DOWNEY, Lawrence M.; B: 1887; D: 1922.
- ELDER, Anselma A.; B: 1848; D: 1918.
- ELDER, Levern Francis; B: 1909; D: 1929.
- FAILENSCHMID, Rev. Julius; B: 1875; D: 1935.
- FUHS, Eva; B: 1861; D: 1907.
- GAYMAN, Anna; B: 1885; D: 3-18-1926.
- GRIFFITH, Ellen; B: 1846; D: 6-18-1905; w/o John.
- GRUND, Frank; B: 1870; D: 12-13-1909.
- GRUND, Monica; B: 1831; D: 1911.
- GUINAN, Louis Edward; B: 8-18-1888; D: 10-3-1898.
- GUINAN, Mary A.; B: 1847; D: 2-8-1915; w/o Thos.
- GUINAN, Thomas; B: 1846; D: 12-31-1920.
- GUINAN, William; B: 1875; D: 1935.
- HAINLEY, Francis W.; B: 1868; D: 1929.
- HAMMES, Frank; B: 1861; D: 1893.
- HAMMES, Susan; B: 1860; D: 1927.
- HEIN, Anna Shoemaker; D: 7-27-1905; w/o Peter.
- HEIN, John P.; B: 11-12-1904; D: 11-1-1934.
- HEIN, John; B: 1867; D: 1-9-1923.
- HEIN, Joseph; D: 12-27-1885; Age 58.
- HEIN, Mary; B: 1877; D: 9-24-1926.
- HEIN, Nicholas; B: 1864; D: 5-14-1882; s/o J. & M.

- HELLER, Mary C.; B: 1850; D: 1894.
- HELLER, Mary; B: 1867; D: 1924.
- HELLER, William; B: 1850; D: 1924.
- HERKENRATH, Gerdrut; B: 1823; D: 5-20-1888.
- HERKENRATH, Joseph; B: 1826; D: 11-7-1896.
- HERKENRATH, Mary; B: 1857; D: 1919.
- HERKENRATH, Mathias; B: 1884; D: 1925.
- HERKENRATH, Peter; B: 1851; D: 1915.
- HERKENRATH, William; B: 1892; D: 1928.
- HORN, Henry; B: 1887; D: 1920.
- HORN, John; B: 1884; D: 1916.
- HUEBNER, --; B: 1853; D: 1931; w/o Albert.
- HUEBNER, "Father"; B: 1843; D: 1928.
- HUEBNER, "Mother"; B: 1853; D: 1931.
- HUEBNER, Albert; B: 1843; D: 1928.
- JACOBS, Margaret; B: 1859; D: 10-24-1924.
- JACOBS, Mathias; B: 1880; D: 5-16-1902.
- JACOBS, Matilda; B: 1888; D: 8-20-1924.
- JACOBS, Nick; B: 1852; D: 12-7-1918.
- KEOGAN, -; D: 5-1-1935; Age 74; His wife [w/o Thomas?].
- KEOGAN, Thomas; (no dates).
- KLEFFMAN, Bernadina; B: 1853; D: 4-11-1930; w/o Fred.
- KLEFFMAN, Fred; B: 1844; D: 12-17-1923.
- KORTH, Anna J.; B: 7-18-1890; D: 9-19-1917.
- KORTH, Jacob; B: 1818; D: 1-1-1898.
- KORTH, Jennie V.; B: 1865; D: 2-9-1887; w/o J.
- KORTH, Katie Gallobith; D: 2-29-1894; Age 27; w/o M.J.
- KORTH, Mary A.; B: 1824; D: 7-12-1894; w/o Jacob.
- KORTH, Mary Leinen; B: 1863; D: 7-4-1889; w/o P.J.
- KORTH, Peter; B: 1847; D: 7-4-1911.
- KRAUTENBERGER, Susana; B: 1861; D: 4-26-1914.
- LEINEN, Anna M.; B: 1873; D: 12-6-1907.
- LEINEN, Anne; B: 1854; D: 1-24-1912; w/o Mathias.
- LEINEN, Constand; B: 1847; D: 1-16-1916.
- LEINEN, Edwin; B: 1913; D: 1921.
- LEINEN, Emma; B: 1867; D: 1897; w/o P.M.
- LEINEN, Gertrude Barbara; B: 1885; D: 9-12-1907.

- LEINEN, Gertrude; B: 1852; D: 3-29-1917.
- LEINEN, Mathias; B: 1817; D: 9-13-1899.
- LEONARD, Ellen; D: 9-14-1893; Age 63; w/o John.
- LEONARD, John; (no dates).
- LeTAL, Anna; D; 1-6-1920; Age 74.
- LeTAL, John; B: 1850; D: 1917.
- MARSH, Amelia; B: 1891; D: 1928; w/o Albert.
- McANDREWS, E.J.; B: 1855; D: 1926.
- McANDREWS, H.W.; B: 12-10-1911; D: 7-5-1932.
- McANDREWS, Hanora Roche; D: 9-25-1897; Age 30; d/o P.&M.
- McANDREWS, John J.; D: 3-28-1936; Age 65.
- McANDREWS, Mary; B: 1834; D: 1922.
- McANDREWS, Patrick; D: 6-14-1891; Age 66.
- MICHELSKI, Cecelia; B: 1891; D: 1931.
- MILLER, Nicholas; D: 1-10-1894.
- MILLER, Susan; D: 1-4-1893; w/o Nicholas.
- MONAHAN, Chas A.; B: 1900; D: 1918.
- MONAHAN, Chas. A.; B: 1863; D: 1923.
- MONAHAN, Honora; B: 1862; D: 1926.
- MONAHAN, John R.; B: 1857; D: 12-16-1914.
- NASH, Arthur W.; B: 1894; D: 4-16-1919; s/o J.M. & Nellie; ψ World War.
- NASH, Bridget; D: 12-28-1901; Age 64; w/o John.
- NASH, John; D: 3-7-1912; Age 82.
- NASH, Michael; B: 1863; D: 3-21-1909.
- NASH, Nellie; B: 1869; D: 4-20-1904; w/o James M.
- NASH, Rosa; D: 11-15-1889; Age 23; w/o M.H.
- NASH, Thomas; B: 1864; D: 1917.
- NELSON, Susan; B: 1837; D: 11-2-1910; w/o T.J.
- NELSON, Thomas J.; B: 1827; D: 7-17-1901.
- NEUBOUER, Gusten; B: 1856; D: 1-22-1891; w/o Michael.
- NEUBOUER, Michael; B: 1844; D: 7-20-1915.
- OHLINGER, "Father"; B: 1848; D: 1926.
- OHLINGER, "Mother"; B: 1857; D: 1927.
- #PAULEY, John Joseph; B: 1898; D: 1929.
- PETERSON. John; B: 1849; D: 1935.
- PHEIFER, John; B: 1852; D: 1933.

- PITSCH, John; B: 1861; D: 1932.
- POWERS, Edward; D: 1-27-1912.
- POWERS, J.F.; B: 1869, Tiffin, Ia.; D: 11-19-1938.
- POWERS, Nora; B: 1838; D: 1924; w/o Richard.
- POWERS, Richard; B: 1837; D: 1-221-1915.
- RATH, Margaret Stein; B: 11-6-1891; D: 4-5-1921; w/o John.
- REINIG, Anna; B: 1876; D: 10-28-1929.
- REINIG, Barbara; B: 1865; D: 1928.
- REINIG, Jacob; B: 1858; D: 1930.
- REINIG, Mathias; B: 1870; D: 3-1-1916.
- SCHMITZ, Mary; B: 1831; D: 1916.
- SCHUMACHER, Jacob; B: 1880; D: 3-16-1923.
- SCHUMACHER, Susanna; B: 1856; D: 2-20-1934.
- SONDAG, Mary; B: 1859; D: 1899.
- SONDAG, Theodore; B: 1850; D: 1925.
- STEIN, John; B: 1854; D: 3-20-1924.
- STEIN, Joseph C.; B: 1908; D: 1935.
- STEIN, Julia A.; B: 1879; D: 2-7-1920; w/o Peter.
- STEIN, Nicholas; B: 1854; D: 1937.
- STEIN, Peter; B: 1823; D: 1-30-1898.
- STEIWER, Margaret; B: 1844; D: 2-23-1916.
- STEIWER, Peter; B: 1831; D: 10-9-1856.
- STINN, Bertha; B: 1896; D: 1928.
- STINN, Casper; D: 6-6-1926.
- STINN, Margaret; B: 1895; D: 1917; w/o J.C.
- STINN, Mary; B: 1861; D: 1936.
- THOMAS, C.W.; B: 1-7-1917; D: 6-20-1935.
- VON TERSCH, Carl M.; B: 1851; D: 1930.
- WALKER, Andrew D.; B: 1837; D: 8-20-1908.
- WEAR, Michael; D: 8-25-1909; Age 75.
- WEHR, "Father"; B: 1852; D: 1913.
- WEHR, "Mother"; B: 1857; D: 1918.
- WEHR, Nicholas; B: 1882; D: 1897.
- WEHR, Paul; D: 1896.
- WIESE, Julius; B: 1859; D: 1928.
- WIESE, Peter; B: 1886; D: 1912.
- WIESE, Jonny; B: 1906; D: 1933.

- WIESE, Julia; B: 1863; D: 1934.
- WINNING, Albert; B: 1841; D: 1-28-1902.
- WINNING, Gertrude; B: 1847; D: 12-9-1924.

St. Peter's Cemetery

AKA: Saints Peter and Paul Catholic Cemetery.
Located in Defiance in Union Township, Section 13/14. Cemetery is in the western part of Defiance, east of US-59, north of Main Street .

- BOOK, John; B: 1857; D: 1932.
- BOOK, Odelia; B: 1868; D: 1932; w/o John.
- COENON, Christina; B: 1857; D: 1937; w/o John Sr.
- DOTZLER, Joseph; B: 1869; D: 1934.
- ECKERMAN, Anna C.; B: 1855; D: 1937; w/o Lewis.
- ECKERMAN, Hilda; B: 1900; D: 1929; w/o Henry.
- ECKERMAN, Lewis J.; B: 1848; D: 1927.
- ENGELDINGER, Peter; B: 1855; D: 1928.
- GOERES, Mary; B: 3-17-1903; D: 2-6-1928.
- GORSCHE, John; B: 1844; D: 1930.
- HENNSE, C.J.; B: 1885; D: 1916.
- HOFER; Joseph; B: 1861; D: 1927.
- JACOBY, Peter; B: 1878; D: 1933.
- KIRCHBAUM, Mayme M.; B: 1899; D: 1922.
- KIRCHBAUM, Reiner; B: 1859; D: 1937.
- KLEIN, Andrew; B: 1878; D: 1929.
- KLOEWER, Anton; B: 1867; D: 11-16-1922.
- KLOEWER, Barbara; B: 1874; D: 1-8-1928; w/o Anton .
- KOBOLD, Michael; B: 1864; D: 1926.
- KRAMER, C.M.; (no dates).
- KRAMER, Raymond; (no dates).
- KRIER, Marie; B: 8-15-1902; D: 2-13-1931.
- LOEHR, Quinn; B: 1874; D: 1918.
- LOEHR, Rose; B: 1873; D: 1933; w/o Quinn.
- MAJERUS, John; B: 1849; D: 1928.
- MARTENS, Mary; B: 1861; D: 1917; w/o Anton Sr.

- MILLER, Anna M.; B: 1877; D: 4-9-1915; w/o Peter.
- MUENCHRATH, Chris J.; B: 1870; D: 1932.
- MUENCHRATH, Ralph J.; B: 1924; D: 1932.
- QUINN, Anna; B: 1869; D: 5-21-1918; w/o Frank.
- QUINN, Daniel; B: 1842; D: 1925.
- QUINN, Mary Frances; B: 1848; D: 1922; w/o Daniel.
- QUINN, William; B: 12-18-1898; D: 5-21-1936; s/o T.E. & Annie.
- RICKELMAN, Helen; B: 1891; D: 1922.
- ROSMAN, Hoper Leona; B: 1897; D: 1920.
- SCHABEN, Annie; B: 1866; D: 1934; w/o Adolph.
- SCHABEN, Edith M. Kebold; B: 1907; D: 1933; w/o Tony.
- SCHEURING, Susanna; B: 1878; D: 1933.
- SCHLEIER, Katherine; B: 1875; D: 1924; w/o Math.
- SCHLEIER, Math; B: 1866; D: 1935.
- SCHLEIER, Wilhelmina; B: 1879; D: 1936.
- SCHLEIMER, Anton; B: 1869; D: 1936.
- SCHMUETTGEN, Maria Weiland; B: 1858; D: 1923.
- SCHUMACHER, Thomas; B: 1886; D: 1932.
- VON TERSCH, Marie; D: 6-12-1932; d/o Frank & Bertha.
- WELLS, John; B: 1900; D: 1938.
- WORRELL, Isaac C.; B: 1872; D: 1916.
- ZERSCHLING, Frank; B: 1901; D: 1930.
- ZERSCHLING, Josephean; B: 1872; D: 1914.

Washington Township Cemetery

Located near Panama in Washington Township, Section 22. Cemetery is west of Railway Street, north of Park Avenue, on the south side of 1600th Street.

- ADAMSON, James; D: 4-3-1889; Age 82.
- ALBERTUS, -- [Maria?]; D: 5-[1887] ; Age 68; w/o Frederick)
- ALBERTUS, Frederick; D: 6-9-1889; Age 67.
- ASSMAN, Anton; B: 1900; D: 1935.
- BLAIR, Elizabeth A.; B: 1842; D: 4-5-1900.
- CANDEE, George; Age 80; ψ Co.B 12th Ia. Inf.

- CHAMBERLAIN, Arthur Benj.; B: 1867; D: 4-28-1935.
- CHAMBERLAIN, Edwin R.; B: 1838; D: 9-20-1899.
- CHAMBERLAIN, Fred; B: 1857, Pink Rock, Ogle Co., Ill.; D: 7-15-1910, Avoca; h/o Lizzie [H]einke; Avoca Journal Herald.
- CHAMBERLAIN, Melvina M.; B: 1846; D: 1899; w/o Sam'l.
- CHAMBERLAIN, Samuel Sweel [Sewell]; B: 1839; D: 1923.
- COLBURN, Geo. W.; B: 1849; D: 1-17-1901.
- COLBURN, Harriet M.; B: 1822; D: 1-12-1903; w/o Wm.
- COLBURN, Henry C.; B: 1846; D: 7-16-1928.
- COLBURN. William; B: 1823; D: 2-24-1907.
- COLLINS, David; D: 2-12-1902.
- COLLINS, Elise M. Wade; B: 1837; D: 1920; w/o David.
- CRANDALL, Benjamin; D: 3-27-1872.
- CRANDALL, Daniel; D: 12-16-1896; Age 49.
- CRANDALL, Ellen; B: 1838; D: 12-31-1903; w/o Ozonder.
- CRANDALL, George; D: 8-21-1905.
- CRANDALL, Ozonder; B: 1836; D: 11-14-1909.
- CRANDALL, Rebecca; D: 1-9-1894; Age 71.
- CROWDER, Mary M. Puckett; B: 1889; D: 11-5-1911; w/o C[S?].S.
- CROWDER, Rosine; B: 1851; D: 2-18-1930.
- CROWDER; John M.; D: 9-7-1888; Age 37.
- CRUTCHFIELD, Catjerine; B: 1801; D: 3-6-1839.
- DAGGETT, Samuel; B: 1831; D: 4-20-1908.
- ECKLEY, W.H.; B: 1850; D: 4-24-1889.
- GOODALE, Mary; B: 1833; D: 8-27-1898.
- GRAVES, Z.H.; D: 4-11-1893; Age 75; ψ 3rd Ia. Batt.
- HALLADAY, John; B: 1822; D: 6-8-1904; h/o Mary J.
- HALLADAY, Mary J.; B: 1833; D: 12-31-1888.
- HART, Fanny C.; B: 1826; D: 1912.
- HART, Jerome W.; B: 1825; D: 1890.
- HAWLEY, Aaron; D: 10-2-1870; Age 42.
- HAWLEY, Elizabeth; D: 12-15-1879; Age 39.
- HENSTREET, "Father"; B: 1825; D: 1902.
- HENSTREET, "Mother"; B: 1829; D: 1911.
- HERSEY, John; D: 3-7-1910; Age 59.
- HERSEY, Susan; D: 4-5-1920; Age 65; w/o John.
- HILL, Elizabeth; D: 5-25-1893; Age 26; w/o W.S.

- HINKLE, Elizabeth; B: 1813; D: 3-11-1880; w/o Jacob.
- HINKLE, Jacob; B: 1808; D: 2-4-1899.
- KELLEY, Sarah A.; D: 3-17-1899; w/o A.
- KINBROUGH, L.D.; B: 1871; D: 2-1-1921.
- KLEEB, Barbara; B: 1833; D: 1-23-1913; w/o John.
- KLEEB, John; D: 12-6-1898; Age 76.
- LANDAKER, Lawrence H.; D: 7-3-1891; Age 73.
- MAYSENT, Geo. F.; B: 1856; D: 92-4-1913 [13-9-1913].
- NICHOLSON, Eddie; B: 1869; D: 6-28-1890.
- NICHOLSON, Eunice; B: 1834; D: 3-2-1911.
- NICHOLSON, Norman; B: 1823; D: 10-30-1886.
- NICKERSON, Anna E.; [no dates]; w/o Otto.
- NICKERSON, Mary E.; D: 1-15-1891; Age 56; w/o J.R.
- OSBAHR, Heinrich; D: 3-29-1890; Age 37.
- REEDER, Norman; D: 4-2-1934; Age 63.
- REYNOLDS, Roseanna; D: 5-29-1907; Age 71; w/o Wm.
- REYNOLDS, Tessa E.; D: 5-29-1907; Age 71; d/o Wm. & R.
- REYNOLDS, William Y.; B: 1838; D: 7-31-1902; Ψ Civil War
- ROLSTON, Libbie S.; B: 1852; D: 12-19-1902.
- ROUNDY, Mary L.; B: 1871; D: 7-2-1909.
- SINGLETON, Aaron; D: 10-1-1887; Age 70.
- SMITH, Lieusetta C.; D: 3-31-1889; Age 30; w/o L.C.
- TARKINGTON, H.A.; D: 1884; Age 84.
- THEILEIS, Kastena; B: 1830; D: 12-12-1891.
- THILEIS, Henry W.; B: 1847; D: 5-12-1903.
- WEATHERILL, Maria; B: 1834; D: 2-22-1923; w/o Thos.
- WEATHERILL, Thomas; B: 1829; D: [1902].
- WICKS, William J.; D: 3-1-1893; Age 47.
- WILLIAMS, Almiron S.; B: 1861; D: 4-25-1907.
- WILLIAMS, Marth[a]; D: 12-1-1859; Age 62; w/o James.
- WOODARD, Coralie M.; D: 12-28-1910; Age 32; w/o A.
- WOODARD, James E.; B: 1871; D: 1919.
- WOODARD, Mason A.; B: 1842; D: 12-1-1921.
- WOODARD, Rosina; B: 1867; D: 1927; w/o James.
- WOODARD, Sarah A.; B: 1839; D: 2-5-1928.

Other Burials

Cemetery not indicated or burial outside Shelby County.

- #ABBOT, S.D; D: 8-13-1909; Age 74; Res. Shelby, Ia.; Avoca Journal-Herald, 8-19-1909 [no cemetery listed].
- #ALLENTZEN, George; B: 1849; D: 2-24-1914; Age 65; Res Harlan; Des Moines Register Leader, 2-25-1914.
- CARLSON, Carl H.; B: 1878, Denmark; D: 12-22-1913; Died on farm near Harlan [no cemetery listed].
- CHRISTENSEN, Jens Christian; B: 1879, Denmark; D: 2-25-1923; Wife, Nor[?]; (burial record Harlan); (Avoca Journal-Herald); [no cemetery listed].
- HEINE, Dora Lutt; B: 1847; D: 10-31-1909; Buried 3 mi east of Shelby.
- HEINE, Henry; B: 1840; D: 6-12-1922; h/o Dora Lutt; Buried 3 mi east of Shelby.
- HEINE, Charlie; B: 1872; D: 11-6-1893; s/o D. & H.; Buried 3 mi east of Shelby, res.
- #HOWARD, Clyde; B: 7-19-1891; D: 10-15-1918. Burial Record from Neola Gazette Reporter 10-24-1918. [no cemetery listed].
- KOHNOP, Herman; D: 8-12-1895; Res. Shelby, Ia., Waverly Independent, 8-15-1895; [No cemetery listed - Shelby?].
- LANGSETT, Harold; D: 5-1-1936; Age 41; Res. Harlan; h/o Myrtle Poole; Cedar Rapids Gazette Reporter, 5-7-1936; [no cemetery listed - Harlan?].
- LOEZ, John; D: 9-26-1905; Age 60; Res. Harlan, Ia. [no cemetery listed - Harlan?].
- LUTT, Katharine; D: 5-11-1991; Age 35; w/o Carl; Buried 3 mi. e of Shelby.
- NICOLAI, Chris Sr.; B: 1851, Germany; D: 12-29-1930; h/o Mary Fixel; Valley Creek Cemetery [Delaware Co., Ia.].
- NORMAN, Michael; D: 2-10-1837, Clarke Co.; Osceola (Ia.) Murray News 2-12-1837. [no cemetery listed].
- PAULSEN, Chas.; D: 10-5-1908; Res. Harlan, Ia.; Avoca Journal-Herald; [no cemetery listed - Harlan?].
- PHILLIPS, Cathrina; B: 1839; D: 5-9-1923. [No cemetery listed].

- REINIG; John K.; (no dates); Ψ Died & buried in France in World War.
- SAYRE, A.H.; D: 11-11-1931; Age 80; Guthrie County Guthrian, 11-12-1931. [no Cemetery listed]
- SLAUGHTER, W.B.; D: 8-12-1935; Age 64; Avoca Journal Herald, 8-15-1935. [no cemetery listed].
- STEWART, Thos. Marion; B: 1838, McConnelsville, Ohio; D: 9-24-1908, Stanley Co., S.D.; h/o Laura Vinson; (Burial record). [No cemetery listed].